Eucharist!

An Eight-Session Ritual-Catechesis Experience for Adults

Susan S. Jorgensen

Resource Publications, Inc.
San Jose, California

Editorial director: Kenneth Guentert
Managing editor: Elizabeth J. Asborno
Illustrations: George Collopy

For permission to reprint any other part of this book, write to:

Reprint Department
Resource Publications, Inc.
160 E. Virginia Street #290
San Jose, CA 95112-5876

ISBN 0-89390-293-4

Printed in the United States of America

98 97 96 95 94 | 5 4 3 2 1

to all the faith-filled people who participate in this program

Contents

Acknowledgments

Grateful acknowledgement is made to the copyright holders who granted permission to reprint the following:

Excerpts from the English translation of *Lectionary for Mass* © 1969, 1981, International Committee on English in the Liturgy, Inc. (ICEL); excerpts from the English translation of *The Roman Missal* © 1973, ICEL; excerpts from the English translation of *Documents on the Liturgy, 1963-1979: Conciliar, Papal, and Curial Texts* © 1982, ICEL. All rights reserved.

Excerpts are taken from **Music in Catholic Worship** Copyright © 1983 United States Catholic Conference, 3211 4th Street, NE, Washington, DC 20017. All rights reserved.

Excerpts are taken from **Environment and Art** Copyright © 1978 United States Catholic Conference, 3211 4th Street, NE, Washington, DC 20017. All rights reserved.

Excerpts are taken from **Liturgical Music Today** Copyright © 1982 United States Catholic Conference, 3211 4th Street, NE, Washington, DC 20017. All rights reserved.

Scripture selections are taken from the **New American Bible** Copyright © 1970, **New American Bible With Revised New Testament** Copyright © 1986, and **New American Bible Revised Psalms** Copyright © 1991 Confraternity of Christian Doctrine, Inc., 3211 4th Street, NE, Washington, DC 20017 and used with permission. All rights reserved.

Abbreviations used for the documents quoted in this book are as follows:
- ◊ CSL — *Constitution on the Sacred Liturgy*
- ◊ GI — *General Instruction of the Roman Missal*
- ◊ LI — *Lectionary for the Mass: Introduction*
- ◊ EACW — *Environment and Art in Catholic Worship*
- ◊ MCW — *Music in Catholic Worship*
- ◊ LMT — *Liturgical Music Today*
- ◊ DMC — *Directory for Masses with Children*

"Sing of a Blessing" words and music by Sister Miriam Therese Winter Copyright: Medical Mission Sisters, 1982, 1987. Reproduced with permission of copyright owner.

Excerpts reprinted from **FREEDOM: A Guide for Prayer**, by Bergan and Schwan. (St. Mary's Press, Winona, MN 1988). Used by permission of the publisher. All rights reserved.

Excerpts from *Eucharist: Essence, Form, Celebration* by Johannes Emminghaus (The Liturgical Press, 1976). Used by permission.

Excerpt from *The Desert Is Fertile* by Dom Helder Camara copyright ©1974 by Orbis Books (Maryknoll, New York). Used by permission.

My heartfelt thanks go first to Ann Marie Caron, whose course was the inspiration for the program. In a last-minute, eleventh-hour (it was, indeed, 11:00 p.m.) effort, the structure and method took shape. The project I had been working on was going nowhere; the oral presentation was due the following day. Desperation was the operative feeling at that late hour. I shook my hands at the heavens and shouted at God, "This is not working!" It was in that moment that inspiration took over and the program was born. To see the hand of God moving so clearly is truly a moment of grace. Ann has continued to support and encourage me.

Andrée Grafstein was co-presenter for each of the programs that we presented. Her presence is on every page of this manual. We sat for hours at each other's kitchen tables, hunched over sacramentaries, searching Scripture and listening to music for ideas and inspiration, drinking endless cups of tea, praying at times quietly and at times passionately for a sense of where God wanted us to be. We worked side by side for many grace-filled weeks.

My thanks go also to the people who attended the program faithfully. Their input shaped the manual as it is now. Their insights and response touched the innermost places of my soul. I would often come away from a session wondering how much more deeply God could move us all.

Beyond these people, I must thank my gifted, patient, dedicated editor, Liz Asborno, whose thoughts and comments bring greater clarity and organization to nearly every page; I thank Jerry Hall, whose unflagging support helped me to smooth out the rough edges in the manual; I thank Eleanor Bernstein, who reviewed portions of the manuscript and gave me many suggestions and thoughtful input; I thank Mary Blume, who graciously accepted the tedious job of proofreading; I thank those who accepted our proposal to put this program on—Bill Thuer, Brian Jeffries and Maureen McMahon; I thank again my spiritual directors—Mark, Liz, Joe and Tony—whose prayerful presence in my life has enabled me to experience God's presence more clearly and deeply; I thank my friends for believing in me and encouraging me to continue my work—Carol Storey, Mary Espinosa, Bob Burbank, Ken Suibielski, Jean Cardello, Anne Carroll, Joe Marcucio; finally (saving the best for last), a thank you to my family—Jorg, Amy, Matthew and Stacy, who have loved me and put up with the impossibly long hours I have been nearly glued to my computer. Bedtime hugs and kisses and last-minute homework corrections were often illuminated by the familiar light of the computer screen. Were it not for their patience and understanding, this project never would have come to birth.

Preface

A little more than thirty years after Vatican II published its first document, the *Constitution on the Sacred Liturgy*, where are we? How frequently do we encounter and embrace the full, active and conscious participation so eloquently envisioned in that document? Sadly, it is often still an ideal espoused by those in the liturgical field, not a reality experienced by the people in the pew. As in the rest of our lives, we are a people separated from ourselves and from the action of worship. In light of the current state of our cultural and lifestyle choices, this should be neither surprising nor unanticipated.

We are a culture that dwells on a painful precipice I would call separation and isolation. We are separated from ourselves, from our world and often from the God who so loves us. We have become isolated human beings with a weak, often non-existent support system. We turn increasingly to material possessions, an insatiable desire for more, and a rapid pace of living to numb the pain of that reality. We are left with very little time to breathe, let alone to contemplate or pray. In this state of being, our ritual life suffers.

This is not meant to be a scathing condemnation of our society, simply an honest observation. We cannot plan a journey to anywhere or create a methodology for anything if we have not assessed who we are, where we are and what our needs might be. This is as true for those of us who plan a single, two-hour program that unfolds in a church basement or a school hall as it is for those of us who are looking for a sense of where we are to go next with Vatican II and liturgical renewal.

> Ritual maintains the world's holiness....The soul might be cared for better through our developing a deep life of ritual rather than through many years of counseling.
> — Moore 226-227

A Call for a New Focus

Thirty years of "new theology" is not enough to bridge the separation that hundreds of years of "old theology" created in the minds and hearts of those who come to Mass every week: the priest says the prayers and the people watch. In addition to this separation, nothing can kill a liturgy more quickly than the benign neglect or ignorance that often prevails in the carrying out of the movements and rhythms of ritual.

Where do we need to focus our efforts toward liturgical renewal? We need to tend to the interior elements at play during all forms of public prayer: the delicate dance of the human and divine spirit; the intricate rhythms of the soul, alive and on fire in the presence of God.

We need to educate priest and layperson alike in a way that pierces their souls and takes root in their hearts. This is formation in its boldest definition. This formation is the responsibility of both laypeople and clergy, who are integral parts of the same equation, neither of which comes first nor carries more weight or importance than the other.

Tending to the interior elements at play during any celebration of liturgy is a risky venture at best. It is not unlike the effort of planting many seeds with great care and then discovering no timetable for the harvest. It is a very different experience from that of tending to exterior elements. The most important difference is that it is a process, not an isolated event.

Liturgical Renewal As a Process

First, process, by its very nature, may have a definite beginning but will rarely have an end. This particular process is a lifelong spiritual journey with the God who companions and so loves us. The journey demands a marriage of the communal and the personal. Our public prayer is the communal expression of the journey; our private prayer is its personal expression. These two support and enrich each other. An intimate link exists between them, a link that needs to be acknowledged and nurtured.

After the earthquake there was fire—but the LORD was not in the fire. After the fire there was a tiny whispering sound. When he heard this, Elijah hid his face in his cloak...
— 1 Kings 19:12-13

Second, process requires a personal investment and commitment on each person's part. This is where the risk comes in. It is not easy to invite God to be with us in a way that is intimate and revealing. This is a scary proposition for all of us (saints included). No one is free from this experience of fear and we are endlessly creative at finding ways to escape the investment.

Third, process requires a different approach. It is not as simple and straightforward as cost estimates and bid evaluations for a church renovation, which can be computerized and compared. It is not as clearcut as organizing a liturgical procession, selecting a new chair for the presider or attending a refresher course in rubrics (does the deacon kneel or stand during the Eucharistic Prayer)?

Creating a Methodology

This manual develops an approach that supports liturgical renewal as a process. We must begin by acknowledging that we need to do more than simply talk and write about liturgy and its various elements. We must tenderly address the people in prayer—the assembly—and work boldly and openly with the actual liturgical texts and prayers the people in prayer use each time they attend

Mass. These texts are not the private property of the Church insofar as we understand "the Church" to be the hierarchy and governing institution. Nor are the texts the private property of the priest insofar as we understand "the priest" to be the "celebrant" of the liturgy and the only one responsible for it. These texts are the intimate and revealing conversation of an assembled people expressing a deep and profound love to their God, and they are a part of us.

Addressing the assembly and working with the texts in the Sacramentary guarantees that, whatever methodology we develop to support the process, it will be fully real, fully grounded in who we are and what we do. The methodology we embrace must be akin to rolling up our sleeves, digging into and mining the depths of our liturgical experience. We must find courage to ask ourselves the question, "What happens when we pray together?" with an awareness that we will never be in full possession of the answer.

Elements of the Methodology

What methodology might best support this process, might best foster a living liturgical renewal in our midst? One methodology that might serve this goal has four elements:

◊ It must be firmly based, but not limited to, a catechesis that addresses the actual texts we pray, proclaim and hear during every liturgy. The teaching grounds us firmly in tradition and fosters deeper understanding of the liturgical action.

◊ It must encourage us to reflect upon our experience during liturgy; this reflection is again based on the actual liturgical texts. Our reflection deepens, honors and makes the experience more real to us.

◊ It must provide us with opportunities to share that experience within the context of a group we have come to know and trust. Our sharing makes the experience more concrete in a way that nothing else can.

◊ It must help us to learn how to pray with and into the elements of liturgy in a way that is mindful and heartfelt. Our prayer binds us together intimately as members of the Body of Christ.

To commit ourselves to a methodology such as this is to commit to growth and change. It is a commitment to become a "new creation" as we allow our God to move more deeply within us. Becoming a new creation is a promise rooted in the faith and hope that, in Christ, all things are made new. This is God-given grace in action.

This method may create resistance and arouse many questions. At its heart, the method is counter-cultural. Make no mistake about

> So whoever is in Christ is a new creation: the old things have passed away; behold, new things have come.
> — 2 Corinthians 5:17

this. First of all, this method is based on small-group formation and process, not mass appeal. We are not basing "success" on reaching the most people in the shortest amount of time. Second, the methodology is not a "quick fix" and does not pretend to provide instant solutions for the issues facing liturgical renewal today. In a culture that thrives on mass appeal, success, quick fixes, instant solutions and results, this methodology may produce the sense that we are "going against the grain."

We will need courage and a conviction that this method is what we need now if we are to help people enter into the mystery of the liturgy more completely, if we are to resurrect our prayer from a certain death caused by boredom and inattentiveness, if we are to realize the breathtaking promise of a loving God who intimately reveals Godself within every moment of that public prayer.

There is a passion that underlies all liturgical celebrations. It is the tender passion of a God who so loves us. It is the deep passion of a Christ who pours out his life for us. It is the burning passion of our hearts as we allow this love and outpouring to enter into the depths of our being. Embracing this process and using this method, we will become tillers of the soil in which these passions lie, helping people in prayer to become more in touch with who they are and who God is in their everyday lives and in their ritual celebrations.

Lord,
  our help and guide,
make your love the
    foundation of our lives.
May our love for you
    express itself
in our eagerness to do
    good for others.
    —Opening Prayer,
Twenty-Eighth Sunday
    in Ordinary Time

A Few Considerations

About Personal and Communal Experience

From the outset of this program, we need to be clear that there is a difference between private and personal. Our culture tends not only to equate the two but to place a very high value on a type of rugged individualism that has been privatized in the most extreme way. How do we counteract the nearly automatic tendency to privatize the personal and individual? Robert Bellah, in his book *Habits of the Heart*, states that "American individualism is not to be rejected but transformed by reconnecting it to the public realm" (248).

Because personal experience is essential to the process of interiorization, it forms one of the cornerstones of this program. The focus on the personal is not a sanction or call to privatize experience. A healthy focus on the personal is incomplete if it is not situated within and connected to the larger community. A healthy focus on the personal will, by its very nature, lead to a greater sense and appreciation of the communal. In the chapter entitled "Public and Private Moments" in his book *Worship: Praying the Sacraments*, Peter Fink discusses the personal in terms of "content" and the communal in terms of "context" (165-184). His comments point to the intimate connection between the two realms.

By their very nature, the reflections and prayer used in this program draw participants more deeply into the realm of the personal. Recognizing and strengthening the relationship between the personal and the communal is a delicate, necessary part of the process. This program enhances that relationship simply because it relies on the communal realm for its context. All of the components of the program unfold within the community of believers. It could not be otherwise. As presenters, our own experience of the program has been a clear witness to and affirmation of the fact that the personal and the communal elements form an intimate whole. They are part of a both/and equation, not an either/or. The one truly does complete and transform the other.

About Structure

A word about the structure of this program as it relates to the structure of the liturgy. In a perfect world, the way we have structured the program would correspond to the structure of the liturgy. In a perfect world, we would be able to fit all the parts of the Liturgy of the Word into one session. In a perfect world, we would be able to fit the eucharistic prayer into one session and the full communion rite in another. In a perfect world...

Time constraints and process prevent us from exactly matching the structure of this program to the structure of the liturgy. The Liturgy of the Word begins in Session 3 and concludes in Session 4. The Liturgy of the Eucharist spans 3½ sessions. To counteract any confusion that this might create, you will need to clearly explain the structure of the rite to your group. Session 1 includes a Resource Page entitled "Parts of the Mass" expressly for this purpose.

About Inclusive Language

My sense is that we need to stay away from using any pronoun in reference to God. Because God is everything in all of us, it is no more correct to refer to God as "she" as it is to refer to God as "he." While referring to God always as "God" is much less poetic and the word "Godself" often feels less personal, this approach is far more faithful to the reality of God and far more inclusive. For many, referring to God as "he" may be a hard habit to break and yet, given the climate of our culture today, it merits the additional effort. The children in my second-grade religious education class refer often to God as "he" and seldom as "she" and I ponder how this impacts their sense of image and identification. For ourselves and for future generations, we need to make our expressions of God equally accessible to both men and women.

Introduction

This manual is a resource for those who are interested in conducting a program designed to bring about liturgical renewal in your parish/community setting. The manual presents in detail an eight-session program that works in four different ways with the liturgical texts used in our ritual celebration of eucharistic liturgy. These ways are described in Part One: A General Methodology.

We direct this program toward those people who are interested in deepening their own participation in liturgy as well as helping (through example) those around them. The call to do this is of prime importance in the *Constitution on the Sacred Liturgy*.

We hope that your primary goal as a presenter is to help the participants understand and experience a deeper sense of full and active participation. This full and active participation will result in a deeper, more critical commitment on the part of each participant as he/she grows more united in and to Christ and with other participants. This full and active participation will help participants to see themselves more clearly as self-gift to God and others.

What do all these words mean? So often, we get carried away with our theologizing and fancy language. In the end, much of it remains at the "word" level—it looks good on paper but it stops there. Simply put, what we are looking for in our work in ministry are ways to help people let God love them and help them to love God in turn. It is that basic.

Our liturgies embody this love. When we are in touch with the God who so loves us and with the part of ourselves that so loves God, our celebrations resound with song and prayer, participation and commitment. We become passionate about what we do; our words and actions come straight from the heart with grace and energy; we encounter God in the act of ritual!

This is the goal of the program. We will show you many different ways of trying to do this, some of which may work for you and some of which may not. We encourage you to experiment with the material here; use what seems appropriate for your group and discard what does not. We write for both the person who has had much experience working with groups and presenting programs and the person who has not. For the person who has, much of the "how-to" might seem superfluous and unnecessary. Feel free to skip that which feels familiar and breaks no new ground for you. We write in freedom; we ask you to read and respond in freedom as well.

Father in heaven,
words cannot measure
  the boundaries of love
for those born to new life
  in Christ Jesus.
Raise us beyond the limits
  this world imposes,
so that we may be free
  to love as Christ teaches
and find our joy in your
  glory.
        — Alternative
Opening Prayer,
Tenth Sunday
in Ordinary Time

Scheduling the Eight-Session Program

This program is an experience geared toward ongoing liturgical renewal over a long period of time. It is designed to be eight separate 2½-hour sessions. Could you combine several and hold a one-day or weekend workshop? You could, but we have reservations. We believe in "slow but sure" (to quote a time-worn phrase) and in the benefits of what we will call "percolation." Each session is full. If the program is done over several days or perhaps one weekend, participants will have little time for the experience of each session to percolate down into their inner being, to penetrate and begin to work its own particular wonder within each person.

That said, we recognize our bias and invite you to shape the program to fit your individual needs. When and how you schedule these sessions is up to you. We have done it two different ways; you may want to try one of the following.

Option One: Split the eight-session program into two segments. This works quite well, particularly if you declare one academic year (September to May) to be a year of renewal for your community. If you choose to do this, you might want to hold the first four sessions, which focus on the Introductory Rites and the Liturgy of the Word, in the fall. You would then schedule the second four, which focus on the Liturgy of the Eucharist, in the early spring. The fall sessions, which are the birth and celebration of the Word in community, will lead into Advent, which awaits the birth and celebration of the Word in the world. The spring sessions, which celebrate the paschal mystery in all its aspects, will lead into your Easter preparations. The complementarity gently brings your study and your prayer together.

Option Two: You could hold eight consecutive weekly sessions, either in the fall or in the spring, being careful not to interfere with Advent or Easter preparations.

What are the advantages and drawbacks to each option? Some people may find that an eight-week commitment feels too big for lives which are already over-crowded with many different responsibilities. A four-week commitment at two separate times might feel more manageable. The drawback is that you may end up with two different groups of people or at least not the same group. You will also lose some of the momentum and cohesiveness that builds up within the group over a consecutive eight-week experience. This may not be as much of a problem if the parish has made a year-long commitment to liturgical renewal.

> In the reform and promotion of the liturgy, this full and active participation by all the people is the aim to be considered before all else.
>
> — CSL 14

Scheduling Each Session

Each session is designed to last 2½ hours. To give you greater flexibility, we have written the schedules in minutes (ten minutes for this piece, twenty for this, etc.) rather than in specific hours of the day. You may use any timeframe convenient for you, be it morning, afternoon or evening.

The schedule is provided as a guideline only. Please do not write it in concrete or engrave it upon your heart (or hand, as the case might be). You may feel that 2½ hours is too long. If so, shorten (rather than eliminate) the time allotted for each item. It is easiest to shorten the reflection, sharing or teaching times. Done reverently and with mindfulness, we find that the prayer time always takes as long as we have allowed.

Creating Your Session Space

The "session space" is where you will be unless you are in the church building for certain prayers or in a prayer space that you create in lieu of the physical church. Your session space needs to be inviting and welcoming, warm and open. This is not hard to do, even on a meager budget.

◊ We prefer a circle of chairs rather than rows. If your group is very large (and we hope you have no more than twenty!), you can work several nested semi-circles. Anything is better than rows (we don't know anyone who prefers looking at the back of a person's head). If you have more than one presenter, sit next to each other. The coordination is much easier.

◊ Find a small table, drape it with clean linen and place on it a candle and either flowers or some symbol of the current liturgical season.[1] Place the table in the middle of the circle.

◊ Your mindfulness and prayerfulness in this space will transform it into a sacred gathering place in which your program can unfold reverently.[2]

> One should be able to sense something special (and nothing trivial) in everything that is seen and heard, touched and smelled, and tasted in liturgy.
> — EACW 12

---

[1] *Refer to Sourcebook for Sunday and Seasons: An Almanac of Parish Liturgy* (Chicago: Liturgy Training Publications, published annually) for many suggestions for each of the seasons.

[2] For more on mindfulness and prayerfulness, see the chapter entitled "Prayer."

The need now is to live with the new liturgy, to make it increasingly a part of our lives, to understand and celebrate it as both a sign of salvation and a self-expression of the Church.
— Emminghaus vi

Variations on the Program

We have already talked about possible options for running the program, but that was within the context of holding an eight-session program. You may not want to hold the eight-session program for a variety of reasons. Or you may want shorter, less comprehensive sessions. Here we look at other ways to use the material presented in this manual.

If you choose to work with the material in any of these ways, we recommend that you first review Part One: General Methodology, paying particular attention to the method that pertains to the option you have chosen.

Evenings of Prayer

You might consider having an evening of prayer connected with some liturgical event in your parish. Or you might open your monthly liturgy committee/commission meetings with prayer. In either case, you could use any of the prayer sections in the sessions. For the most part, the prayers use song and movement, appeal actively to the concept that we are all ministers, and involve each participant on many levels. They each last about ½-hour.

The names and content of each prayer are as follows:

◊ *Altar Prayer:* Participants pray an antiphonal reading and reverence the altar. This is in Session 1, page 36.

◊ *Prayer of Blessing and Sprinkling:* Participants sing a song of blessing, bless water, sprinkle each other and pray a responsorial blessing. This is in Session 2, page 66.

◊ *Prayer of Preparation for the Word:* Presenter leads participants through a guided meditation that focuses on hearing, seeing, understanding and feeling the Word of God when it is proclaimed. This is in Session 3, page 79.

◊ *Prayer of Belief:* Participants meditate on beliefs that are important to them, write those beliefs down, and respond with a prayer about belief. This is in Session 3, page 84.

◊ *Intercessory Prayer:* Participants identify a personal, communal or world need that is important to them. They pray silently about the need. In pairs, they express the need to the other and pray for the other's need. Returning to the group, each person's need is briefly expressed and prayed for. This is in Session 4, page 98.

◊ *Presentation of Gifts:* Participants meditate on the meaning of gift and sacrifice and present themselves at the altar as self gift to God. This is in Session 4, page 101.

◊ *Prayer with Plate and Cup:* Based on Teilhard de Chardin's "Mass on the World," participants offer prayers over an empty plate and cup. This is in Session 5, page 117.

◊ *Lord's Prayer and Peace Prayer:* Participants pray the Lord's Prayer in a way that invites them to put the prayer in their own words. They also experience the Sign of Peace. This is in Session 6, page 132.

◊ *Taking, Blessing and Breaking of Bread:* Participants pass a loaf of bread around a circle three times. The first time, they take the bread into their own hands; the second time, they bless the bread either silently or out loud, using their own words; the third time, they break the bread. This is in Session 7, page 158.

You could use any one of these prayers to begin your regular (monthly) liturgy committee/commission meetings.

Or you might organize an evening of prayer based on one particular prayer.

Any of the above prayers could work as the content portion of an evening of prayer preceded by introductions, coffee and some initial preparation and followed up by some group process. You might allow twenty minutes or so for coffee and introductions, ½-hour for the prayer, and a ten-minute break followed by faith-sharing that focuses on each person's experience of the prayer.

Using one or more of these prayers, you could organize a series of evenings of prayer (lasting approximately 1½ hours) for your community.

Evenings of Reflection

You might have a series of evenings of reflection, using only the reflection sheets in the sessions. You could use them as they are, which would provide nine sessions of an hour or so, or you could combine them into three or four evenings of two hours (or so).

As with the prayers, you could use them as a beginning for a commission/committee meeting for a year. Most of the reflection sheets require ten or fifteen minutes to answer (they could go longer, too) followed by ten or fifteen minutes to share or process.

The following nine reflections are located in the Resource Sheets section at the end of each session:

◊ Entrance Song *through* Greeting, Session 1, page 45

◊ Penitential Rite *through* Opening Prayer, Session 2, page 68

◊ Profession of Faith, Session 3, page 91

The most powerful experience of the sacred is found in the celebration and the persons celebrating, that is, it is found in the action of the assembly: the living words, the living gestures, the living sacrifice, the living meal.
— EACW 29

The dialogue between God and (God's) people taking place through the Holy Spirit demands short intervals of silence, suited to the assembly, as an opportunity to take the word of God to heart and to prepare a response to it in prayer.

— LI 28

◊ Preparation of the Altar and the Gifts *through* Prayer over the Gifts, Session 4, page 108

◊ Preface *through* Acclamation (Sanctus), Session 5, page 122

◊ First Epiclesis *through* Memorial Acclamation, Session 5, page 125

◊ Anamnesis *through* Great Amen, Session 6, page 140

◊ Breaking of the Bread *through* Prayer after Communion, Session 7, page 164

◊ Concluding Rite, Session 7, page 170

Presentations on the Liturgy

Working with only the intent sheets, you could work with a group whose focus is to learn more about liturgy as a ritual—its history, symbols, organization, and some of the Vatican II documents that pertain to liturgy. As with the prayer sheets and reflection sheets, you could use each intent sheet separately to begin your liturgical commission/committee meetings. You could also combine the material and hold three or four two-hour sessions, allowing time for introductions, coffee and a question-and-answer period.

The following eleven intent sheets are located in the Resource Sheets section at the end of each session:

◊ Entrance Song *through* Greeting, Session 1, page 48

◊ Penitential Rite *through* Opening Prayer, Session 2, page 71

◊ First Reading *through* Homily, Session 3, page 88

◊ Profession of Faith, Session 3, page 92

◊ General Intercessions, Session 4, page 106

◊ Preparation of the Altar and the Gifts *through* Prayer over the Gifts, Session 4, page 110

◊ Preface *through* Acclamation (Sanctus), Session 5, page 123

◊ Eucharistic Prayer I — Session 6, page 142

◊ Lord's Prayer *through* Sign of Peace, Session 6, page 153

◊ Breaking of the Bread *through* Prayer after Communion, Session 7, page 167

◊ Concluding Rite, Session 7, page 172

If you choose to use the intent sheets in ½-hour segments (for example, as the beginning of your commission/committee meetings), we recommend combining the following:

◊ First Reading *through* Homily

   with

◊ Profession of Faith

   and

◊ General Intercessions

◊ Preparation of the Altar and the Gifts *through* Prayer over the Gifts

   with

◊ Preface *through* Acclamation (Sanctus)

◊ Breaking of the Bread *through* Prayer after Communion

   with

◊ Concluding Rite

Additionally, the sessions offer recommendations for supplementary material to augment the shorter intent sheets.

This variation would probably be the least effective alternative to using the manual as a whole because it does not address the areas of our faith that so desperately need addressing—mindful communal prayer and the ability to be more aware of our experiences and the God who is so present within all of them.

Identifying Your Audience

Keep in mind that many Catholics have had very little training or education about liturgy, unless they are involved in professional ministry on some level. Even then, the chances that they have had much training in liturgy is unlikely. The idea of liturgical formation for lay, religious, and even, to an extent, the ordained is still a novel one. Up until now, we have made a great many assumptions and relied heavily on the concept of osmosis to communicate what liturgy is all about. This works to a degree—good modeling is a form of osmosis—but it cannot be the sole method of communication.

Particular groups in your community might gravitate toward a program such as this: lectors, ushers, communion ministers, music ministers, cantors and religious education teachers. Because they are involved in liturgy and/or education, they will clearly benefit from what is being presented in this program.

> Priests, both secular and religious, who are already working in the Lord's vineyard are to be helped by every suitable means to understand ever more fully what it is they are doing in their liturgical functions.
> — CSL 18

> I, the LORD,...have grasped you by the hand;
> I formed you, and set you as a covenant of the people,
> a light for the nations.
> —Isaiah 42:6

A second group to consider is the parents of children involved in first communion and confirmation preparation. Liturgy forms a critical part of this preparation, particularly with first communion. Although many changes will be coming regarding these sacraments of initiation, most communities still prepare young school-age children for first communion and adolescents for confirmation. Their parents would benefit greatly from the opportunity to explore liturgy in greater depth.

A third group is the newly baptized, those who have participated in the Rite of Christian Initiation of Adults. The seven Sundays of the Easter Season might be the perfect time to hold this program for them as part of the mystagogia process.

> Among the symbols with which liturgy deals, none is more important than this assembly of believers.
> — EACW 28

Beyond those particular groups, all parishioners and members of your community could be encouraged to attend. Due to the basic nature of the program (it makes no assumptions and has no prerequisites), it is suitable for anyone with even a mild interest in liturgy and prayer. A person can participate in the program on many different levels.

The program could also form the backbone of a diocesan-wide plan for liturgical renewal. Directors of offices for worship and chairpersons of diocesan liturgical commissions could present the program, or they could train others to present it at the parish or deanery level.

One critical question to ask yourself as you begin to identify your audience is, "How many participants would be ideal?" We would love to say as many as want to come (hoping, of course, for numbers to swell the church hall or parish center), but we do not believe this to be the case. If there are two of you presenting the program, we think twelve to sixteen is an ideal number. A group of this size can be broken into two groups of six or eight, either of which is a good number for small group sharing. It is also a workable size for group prayer—not too big, not too small. (This is beginning to sound like *The Three Bears*!) We would advise you to think seriously about having a cut-off limit of sixteen. Beyond twenty, the group becomes cumbersome during group prayer.

> Let all the nations gather together, let the peoples assemble!
> —Isaiah 43:9

Inviting Participants

First and foremost, rely on word of mouth. Talk to people about your program; personally invite them to come. This type of outreach goes a long way and it makes people feel wanted. Prior to the program, ask people for help with advertising—posters, fliers, perhaps telephone calls to a few good candidates. The more enthusiasm you can generate prior to the program, the more successful and well-attended the program will be.

Mail letters to your targeted audience. If you are in a parish, you may want to send letters to all who are involved in the church ministries.

You might ask your pastor to write a cover letter supporting the program and urging people to attend. You may want to send letters to the parents of the children who are preparing for first communion and confirmation. Direct mailing is a good start; it is a lot of work, so ask people for help. Involve your director of religious education; perhaps the program could be a joint effort between the education and liturgy committees. You may want to contact your diocesan liturgy commission or office for worship for information, assistance or coordination.

If you are in a diocesan liturgy office, you may want to send letters to parish liturgy committee chairs. If you do not have a list of those people, send the letter addressed simply to the Parish Liturgy Committee Chair, c/o (parish name). This is less personal, but it will get your message across. If you run the program as a follow-up to the *Rite of Christian Initiation of Adults* (RCIA), use those mailing lists or contact the RCIA coordinators in each parish. You may want to coordinate your efforts with either the diocesan religious education or spirituality/spiritual life office. Ask your bishop/archbishop/auxiliary bishop for support and backing.

Other avenues to explore are the following:

◊ Weekly parish bulletins: an announcement that runs for several weeks and/or a small (one to two paragraphs) article describing the program. Advertise in surrounding parish bulletins as well.

◊ Diocesan newspapers: perhaps an article or press release

◊ Diocesan calendar

◊ Fliers or posters posted on parish bulletin boards or in various diocesan offices, local Catholic colleges and universities

> For the celebration of the eucharist is the action of the whole Church;... these people are the people of God, purchased by Christ's blood, gathered together by the Lord, nourished by his word.... (T)hey are a people growing together into unity by sharing in Christ's body and blood....holy by their origin, but becoming ever more holy by conscious, active, and fruitful participation in the mystery of the eucharist
> — GI 5

Part
One

GENERAL METHODOLOGY

(I)t is critically important for the Church to reemphasize a more total approach to the human person by opening up and developing the non-rational elements of liturgical celebration: the concerns for feelings of conversion, support, joy, repentance, trust, love, memory, movement, gesture, wonder.
— EACW 35

This program uses an approach based on models developed by Gilbert Ostdiek in his book *Catechesis for Liturgy* and Gregory Manly and Anneliese Reinhard in their book *The Art of Praying Liturgy*. Both models involve three phases: attending, reflecting and responding.

◊ *Attending* develops the art, skill, and awareness of each participant's presence at liturgy.

◊ *Reflecting* develops the art of drawing out each person's experience of liturgy.

◊ *Responding* develops the process of deepening commitment based on meaning that has been enhanced through attending and reflecting.

This program builds on these models. We will use four basic components in this program:

◊ *Reflection:* Each person will be asked to reflect on his/her experience during liturgy through a series of reflection questions based on the actual texts we use during our liturgies.

◊ *Group Process:* Generally, after each reflection period, there will be time for sharing in twos, threes, small and large groups.

◊ *Intent:* Each session involves a catechetical element. We call this the "intent" portion of the program and, as with the reflection portion, it is based on the actual texts we use during our liturgies.

◊ *Prayer:* The group will pray together during a part of every session. For about half an hour, participants will pray with certain symbols, actions or liturgical texts that pertain to the part of the liturgy with which a particular session deals.

Reflecting on Experience:
Exploring and Naming Feelings, Meanings, Beliefs

This portion of the program is geared toward helping participants explore what they experience during the various parts of the Mass. This exploration will also help them become more aware of how their participation in the Mass imparts meaning and either strengthens or challenges their beliefs.

Getting Organized

Each session has its own reflection sheets, which are laid out in two columns: the liturgical text is in the left-hand column and the reflection questions are in the right-hand column. Interspersed in the liturgical text you will find numbers in parentheses. The reflection questions are numbered as well. The numbers in the liturgical text refer you to the number of the appropriate reflection question. At this point, you may want to turn to one of the reflection sheets in one of the sessions to get a feel for this structure.

Facilitating the Process

During this time of reflection, a reverent quiet should be established and nurtured. Your own respect for silence will serve as a model for those in your group. In our culture, we Americans do not enter or keep silence well, and we need good modeling. During the reflection period, you may want to play quiet instrumental music. Many good tapes today have been made for the purpose of nurturing quiet reflection and meditation. Playing a tape also eliminates some of the normal background noise associated with any gathering. Stomach rumblings and intermittent coughing, shuffling feet and shifting bodies blend into the gentle background voices of piano and flute.

Before distributing the reflection sheets, it may be helpful to explain two things to participants. First, explain that they may find that they have no answers and that they may find this process difficult and frustrating simply because they have not thought about the Mass in this way before. There are no right or wrong answers to the questions; there are no grades. This is an exercise in looking within ourselves and becoming more aware. Encourage participants to be as free, honest and reflective as they are able to be. Also encourage them to suspend inner judgment of their responses—the universal

---

Presenter's Reflection Questions

As you prepare for or review the reflection part of each session, you might ponder or bring to prayer the following questions:

◊ During your own periods of reflection, what has the process been like for you?

◊ What helps you to be quiet and reflective?

◊ What helps you to quiet your own inner voice of judgment?

◊ When has the reflection process been helpful to you? When has it been frightening, difficult or boring?

As we relive our experience and try to name it for ourselves, we begin to explore more fully what our experience can tell us about ourselves and our world.
— Ostdiek 18

Not that of ourselves we are qualified to take credit for anything as coming from us; rather, our qualification comes from God, who has indeed qualified us as ministers of a new covenant, not of letter but of spirit; for the letter brings death, but the Spirit gives life.
— 2 Corinthians 3:5-6

What was the reflection portion of the program like for you?

It focused my thoughts on parts of the Mass that I had just skipped right over previously....It really forced me to see the words.
— A Participant

parent voice that likes to tell us when we are doing well or poorly or what we should think or feel.

Second, invite people to remember a specific liturgy when the part on which they are about to reflect was particularly meaningful, moving, memorable, touching for them. For example, during Session 1, "Entrance Song *through* Greeting," you might ask them to remember a particular procession or a favorite gathering song. You might ask them to picture themselves in their usual pew or place in the assembly. Encourage them to be in that moment. This can be done effectively in an abbreviated form of a guided meditation. Suggest to them that they remember smells, images, words, music or movement around the memory.

When you feel that the participants have had enough time to do the remembering, distribute the reflection sheets. Ask the participants to read the liturgical texts prayerfully and encourage them to either form mental answers or actually write out responses to the questions, whichever is more comfortable for them. Emphasize this point because many people may feel that they have to write answers, and this is not the intent. Some participants may feel like drawing an image, etc., as a response to a particular question. Encourage people from the beginning to be free to go where the Spirit might lead them. Developing and nurturing inner freedom is important to this program.

Group Process:
Sharing Personal Reflections, Discussing Pertinent Issues

Group process can work in any number of ways. We suggest that you use all of them, depending on the needs and structure of your particular group. Fostering the degree of trust that is necessary for open, honest sharing is a delicate process that depends in part on you and in part on the people in your group. Some people just naturally share more easily than others.

Establishing Guidelines

The first step is to set several guidelines for group process. You may have your own ideas along that line that come from your own experience. If not, consider the following:

◊ Each person should be encouraged to share. Be sensitive yet challenging to those who seldom share; often they just need to be drawn out a little, but that will involve an assessment on your part. Be gentle yet firm with those who tend to go on and on.

◊ All responses should be honored and respected. Most responses need only to be heard and reverenced; comment back is usually unnecessary.

◊ Discourage negative comments, giggling or laughter when it is sarcastic or disrespectful of others. These responses are inappropriate in group process and will kill the process.

◊ Everything shared in the group is confidential. This is critical and anyone who does not honor this guideline should be spoken to as soon as possible.

Types of Group Process

There are many types of group process. We relied on two: group sharing and general discussion.

Group Sharing

We define "group sharing" as a time in which people share their own experience with each other in different sizes of groups (see below for a description of these group sizes). For people who have not done much group work (and it is work!), you will need a trial period during

---

Presenter's Reflection Questions

As you prepare for or review the group process part of each session, you might ponder or bring to prayer the following questions:

◊ What has been your overall sense of the group during any given experience of group process?

◊ What changes are you noticing in the group as you move into the latter sessions of the program?

◊ Have you tried to include each person in the group in the sharing?

◊ Are there certain individuals in the group with whom you have encountered some difficulty or dislike? What might help you to resolve your feelings?

which people feel their way through the process. As the group members become more comfortable with one another, this process will reflect the growing bond and intimacy between them. As was stated above, this will depend on your ability to establish the necessary trust level within the group and their willingness to trust.

General Discussion

General discussion is a second type of group process, wherein the floor is opened up but not limited to questions and general comments that pertain generally to the reflection questions. This combination of teaching and sharing is less formal than the intent section of the program (covered in the next chapter) or a group sharing of personal experience. We often title it, "A-thousand-and-one questions you have been dying to ask but never did." It can be fun, light-hearted, informative and casual. It helps knit the group together; its value cannot be underestimated.

Group Sizes

Group sizes can vary, depending on your needs and preferences:

◊ **Diads or triads:** Two- and three-person groups work well especially if your whole group is greater than ten in number. You may want to switch the members of each group every so often (at least once over the course of the eight sessions) so that different people get to know each other. You can begin by setting the groups up according to proximity—those sitting next to each other form the groups.

◊ **Small groups:** If your whole group is large (greater than ten), you may want to form several smaller groups from time to time, four to six per group. People often find working in small groups more comfortable than working in either diads or in the whole group of ten or more.

◊ **Whole group:** This works well for several different occasions. We have used it mainly when diads/triads or small groups share with the whole group and when the group process is going to be general discussion rather than group sharing.

Facilitating Group Process

Some weeks have many reflection questions and other weeks do not. When the small groups share the reflection questions, it might be best to let each small group pick and choose which questions it will

What was the group sharing portion of the program like for you?

It encouraged me to deepen my love for the Eucharist....I must say I found it most enlightening to learn that we have the same needs and thoughts and aspirations....I'm not so strange and I'm not the only one with questions—something that always surprises me....It was an experience of the presence of God.
— A Participant

share. When the whole group shares and there are many questions, it might be best if, before the reflection begins, you pick several (three or four) that seem the most significant for your group. Let the group know that these are the significant questions and that they might want to answer them first.

The sharing in a group (other than in diads or triads) can be done randomly, allowing anyone to speak when they are so moved. Sharing can also be done methodically, going around the circle in order, with the option to pass if a person does not wish to share. Both methods work and each has advantages and disadvantages. Random sharing is less formal but it can be more awkward—people are often unsure when to speak and long silences can arise. Silence in the presence of others has not been a significant part of our culture or our socialization process and we have a desire (need?) to fill the silence with something. Random sharing is also more difficult for those who are less outgoing. They often simply do not speak. Ordered sharing is more formal and people may feel more pressured if they do not feel free to pass. It is up to you, the presenter, to ensure that the option to pass is truly an option.

In ordered sharing with the whole group, people frequently have the same thoughts, ideas, feelings and experiences. People often say that others before them have said what they would have said. Nonetheless, encourage these people to express their experience in their own words. It is important for people to hear their own words out loud. Vocalization is a significant part of the sharing process.

When general discussion rather than sharing seems appropriate, we will suggest topics for those discussions. As presenter, you must be very careful that these discussion periods do not degenerate into whining, gossipy-type sessions about what Father or the deacon or the DRE or the parish secretary or the music director does or does not do. This type of discussion will not enhance the program; this is not the time or the place to air personal gripes or grievances.

They devoted themselves to the teaching of the apostles and to the communal life, to the breaking of bread and to the prayers....All who believed...had all things in common;...
— Acts 2:42,44

Intent:
Looking at Each Part of the Liturgy— Perspectives from History and Vatican II

The intent portion of the program is primarily instructional. It is designed to help participants understand what the liturgical celebration is asking of them as well as what is happening during each part of the Mass. This part of each session follows a teaching format, primarily in the form of short presentations with time for questions and answers. This part of every session looks at questions such as:

◊ What are we being asked to do?

◊ Why do we do what we do?

◊ What is the history of some of the words, gestures and actions?

◊ What do the words, gestures and actions mean?

Most of the presentations are approximately twenty minutes long. We have not provided an exact script for the teaching; each person's teaching style and knowledge differ so vastly that we chose to list only the important points to cover during each presentation and the resources that are available for reference. Thus, the intent portion of each session will involve some work on your part.

We have provided intent sheets, which are two-column, similar in format to the reflection sheets: the liturgical text is in the left-hand column and the explanation—the intent—is in the right-hand column. Intent sheets include general comments about each section of the liturgy (Introductory Rites, Liturgy of the Word, Liturgy of the Eucharist, Concluding Rite) as well as comments about specific actions and words. Most of what you will teach is on these sheets. All you will need to do is provide a small amount of supplementation or "filler" material. (We recommend that you distribute copies of the intent sheets to all participants at the end of each session. These sheets are meant to be reference material for them, not something to read or follow along with during your presentations.)

Presenter's Reflection Questions

As you prepare for or review the intent part of each session, you might ponder or bring to prayer the following questions:

◊ What qualities are assets in teaching?

◊ Which of these assets do you perceive in yourself? How might you enhance them?

◊ What is your own experience of and feeling about teaching?

◊ What encourages you to learn and to ask questions?

◊ During any given session, how have you responded to questions and comments?

How was the intent part of the program useful?

It made me more aware of the meaning of the Liturgy in my own life; helped me to bring a more intense feeling of what is really happening to me as a participant.
— A Participant

Prayer:
Providing Time and Space to Encounter God in Liturgy

Liturgy is prayer! It is our intimate longing for and encounter with the God who so loves us. It is our expression of love for God in return for all that God has given to us. Speaking out loud to God in community through ritual is one way of engraving this covenant between God and us upon our hearts for all to see.

Looking at Liturgy As Prayer

How do we pray together in community? The concept that liturgy is prayer is a new one for many of us. Why?

◊ We often miss the sense that liturgy is indeed prayer because liturgy becomes one more thing to do in busy lives that are overwhelmed with things to do. Liturgy becomes simply another chore on the list, waiting to be crossed off upon completion.

◊ The sense that liturgy is prayer also gets buried by the overriding sense that liturgy is an obligation to fulfill. God will "get us" if we don't go; how hard it is for us to shed that fear, and yet how necessary it is to move beyond it. Real communication is difficult at best when the participants are only there because they think they have to be.

◊ The association between liturgy and prayer is lost in part because of our limited definition of prayer as "that which we do in the privacy of our rooms"—three "Our Fathers," two "Hail Mary's," and, on a good night, a rosary (a little insurance goes a long way).

In the prayer portion of each session, you will take at least one specific symbol (in several sessions, there are two prayer experiences) and pray with that symbol. This allows you to stop the liturgy at a specific point and explore that point prayerfully and reverently, with leisure and love. There is no opportunity to do that during the ordinary process of liturgy: At Sunday liturgy, we can't raise our hands and say to the presider, "Can we stop for a moment? I think God is trying to speak to me/us through this symbolic word, object or action" or "Could you slow down just a little?; I/we need more time right now to 'be with' what is happening." Here, you have the time and space.

What was the prayer part of the program like for you?

The prayer experiences were awesome....Praying the "Our Father" was compelling....I felt the spirit prompting not only me but all the others. It was beautiful and from deep within the heart.
— A Participant

Do you not know that your body is a temple of the holy Spirit within you?...Therefore glorify God in your body.
— 1 Corinthians 19,20

The Organization of the Prayers

Each prayer section includes the following elements for you, the presenter:

◊ Introduction

◊ Outline

◊ Presenter Preparation

◊ Details

The introduction situates the prayer for you and sets you within its context. The outline of the prayer enables you to do a walk-through with the participants; before beginning the actual prayer, this brief explanation lets people know what will be happening in what sequence. The presenter preparation is in list form; it suggests the things you need to do and any objects that you might need for the prayer (baskets, candles, etc.). This creates a certain level of comfort and an atmosphere in which prayer can actually happen. The details, we hope, will be thorough and complete.

Preparing Yourself for Prayer

What will help you to facilitate the prayer part of the program? Three things play a key role:

Personal Comfort with Your Body

We use our bodies to pray with, or at least that is the theory. Many of us fall far short of that because we are not comfortable or happy with the way we look. Go to an eighth-grade graduation and watch the children process in if you want to see what happens when we are uncomfortable in and unhappy with our bodies. No amount of preparation can completely eliminate the shuffling and slouching, awkwardness and general lack of grace that abound. It is almost painful to witness.

As presenter, you can model grace with and in your body. Any liturgical action that is performed with grace will be worthy of note and moving to behold: processions, incensing, hand postures, bowing and genuflecting, to mention a few. Done well, your body motion becomes an intimate part of the prayer.

Mindfulness

Especially in prayer, you can model mindfulness. What is mindfulness? It is an awareness of what you are doing in the present moment. It is attentiveness to that activity. It is a sense of intention about what you are doing. It is a reverence you bring to all that you do. The reverence is the birth that springs forth from the awareness, attentiveness and intention.

Students of Buddhism often practice walking, imagining that, with each step they take, they are placing their foot on the head of Buddha. Preparation for international dances of peace often begin by walking in a circle, with an invitation to be aware of what you are doing and how your body feels as you do it, and then to notice changes in your mind, body and spirit as you continue to walk.

There is no limit to mindfulness. Mindfulness is our "I am" to God and to the world around us. It brings fire to the celebration of who we are and of all that God has given to us. We invite you to incorporate mindfulness in all that you do in your program. It will make a difference that is real and tangible.

Prayerfulness

Do not mistake the saying of prayers with the condition of being prayerful. What is prayerfulness? It is so intimately related to mindfulness that it may be impossible to have one without the other. Mindfulness is an awareness of self as we relate to others. Prayerfulness is an awareness of God as God relates to us. Prayer is the language of this awareness.

Prayerfulness is an expression of the heart. It is the act of being grateful for all that we have been given. The more mindful we are, the more aware we become of these gifts. That is why mindfulness and prayerfulness are so intimately linked. We can be prayerful about the simple act of watering our gardens. We can be grateful for the gentle sound of running water as it touches the leaves of the plants; grateful for seeing the droplets of water form, cradled lovingly in the inner recesses of every flower petal and delicately dancing from the tip of every leaf; grateful for the aroma of water and earth, created from the intimate union of the two. Our gratitude for all of these things is our prayerfulness.

As with mindfulness, there is no limit to prayerfulness. Prayerfulness is our "you are" to the God who has created us in God's image and who so loves us. It brings gentle passion—an ache and a longing of the heart—to our celebration of who God is and how much God loves us.

How does this affect you as you carry out this program? You can begin by being grateful for each person who sits with you, grateful for the circle of people who have gathered to grow in their experience of liturgy. Your gratitude can extend to the simple lighting of the candle as you begin the gathering prayer. Your prayerfulness in every action that you do will be noticed by others. It is contagious!

To gather intentionally in God's presence is to gather our total selves, our complete persons—a "living sacrifice."...Liturgy is total, and therefore must be much more than a merely rational or intellectual exercise.
— EACW 35

Good liturgy is people praying well; poor liturgy is when people pray poorly. There is no place for anything, or any person, in a celebration that does not contribute to help the people to pray.
— Manly and Reinhard 22

"Saul, my brother, the Lord has sent me, Jesus who appeared to you on the way by which you came, that you may regain your sight and be filled with the holy Spirit." Immediately things like scales fell from his eyes and he regained his sight.
— Acts 9:17-18

Prayer with Purpose

The prayer is an end in itself, but participants will also carry the experience of this prayer into their celebration of liturgy. What are you specifically striving for in this portion of the program?

◊ The symbols[1] encountered in liturgy will come alive for participants—*alive!*

◊ The participants will see a dimension of these symbols that they never saw before; their vision of liturgy will be renewed. This is an "Aha!" experience—the experience of seeing something for the hundredth time and yet, somehow, seeing it for the very first time.

◊ Through their renewed vision, the participants will grow in their appreciation of and reverence for these symbols.

For us, this portion of the program was a moving experience. The prayer was never the same twice, but it was obvious to all of us that God was present, alive, moving within our community when we took time to pray together.

---

[1] "Symbols" here includes all words, objects, gestures and action that occur within the liturgy.

Part Two

THE
SESSIONS

How the Sessions Are Set Up

Part Two devotes a separate chapter to each session. Each chapter explains everything that you will cover during that particular session, in the order in which it is scheduled for that session. The order varies from session to session: the prayer part is not in the same place every session, nor is the reflection, group process or teaching.

During any given session, the manual will refer to the reflection, intent and prayer sheets to be given to the participants. These sheets are at the end of each session in a section entitled "Resource Sheets." All Resource Sheets are marked with the following icon, which signifies permission to photocopy:

Each of the eight sessions includes the following:

◊ Schedule

◊ Resource Sheets

◊ Recommended Reading — suggestions for supplementary reading for the participants. If you find the articles worthwhile, you might want to ask for reprint permission and copy them for the people in your program.

◊ Overview

◊ Presenter's Reflection Questions

◊ Approach and suggested content for teaching pieces that supplement the intent sheets

◊ Suggestions for additional reading for you, the presenter, which will aid you in your teaching

◊ Format for and content of prayer

◊ Questions for general discussion where applicable

All sessions will include a time of silent reflection, group process and a teaching of intent that addresses the part of the liturgy being covered during that particular session.

Supplementary Resources

We have made suggestions about the main points to be covered in the teaching parts of the program (intent of the liturgical texts as well as some additional teaching sessions). We recommend that you follow the general content on each intent sheet. To supplement that material, we provide a "Recommmended Reading" list, which contains books and articles that expand upon the main points of each sheet.

Written material on liturgy abounds! Many are good and worthwhile, but we recommend these four basic resources (see the "Works Cited and Recommended" section in the back of this book for full bibliographic information):

◊ *The Word and Eucharist Handbook* by Lawrence J. Johnson. This 168-page book is a gem. It walks you through the entire liturgy, providing concise explanations and quotations from the Vatican II documents as they apply. Mr. Johnson presents his research clearly and provides a list of recommended reading for each part of the rite.

◊ *The Eucharist: Essence, Form, Celebration* by Johannes Emminghuas. This thorough, 229-page book is divided into two parts: the first concentrates on the history and development of the Mass; the second describes the current rite in great detail. While Rev. Emminghaus can be wordy at times, your patience will reward you with some interesting bits of information.

◊ *The Liturgy Documents*, published by Liturgy Training Publications. *The Constitution on the Sacred Liturgy* (December 1963) was the first decree of the Second Vatican Council. Many other valuable documents have been printed since this, but the *Constitution* remains the primary source for all that have followed. It is the definitive guide upon which all liturgical reform that flowed from that Council is based. The *General Instruction of the Roman Missal* (4th ed., March 1975) and its Appendix for the Dioceses of the United States is printed at the beginning of every Sacramentary. Other helpful resources include *Environment and Art in Catholic Worship* (1978); *Liturgical Music Today* (1982); *Music in Catholic Worship* (rev. ed. 1983); *Lectionary for Mass: Introduction* (1981).

◊ The Sacramentary (rev. ed. 1985). This edition includes the three Eucharistic Prayers for masses with children and two for masses of reconciliation.

When we refer you to these resources, we will list the pages that are applicable to each particular session. Using these texts, you will build a solid foundation to support your teaching. You may have a favorite resource or two; use those if you prefer. Occasionally, we will suggest a periodical article that is provocative or provides some interesting information regarding the liturgical text being taught in a particular session.

Hiding under the bland cover, buried between the fraying ribbons, (the Sacramentary has) a wonderful collection of prayer texts and worship guidelines ready for the church to use in many settings.

G. T. Ryan 4

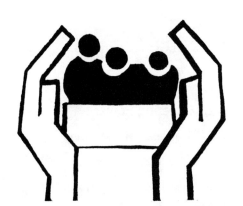

Session 1:
Entrance Song *through* Greeting

God gathers us, the worshiping assembly, into the Body of Christ.

Schedule

Time	Description
5 minutes	Participant Questionnaire
10 minutes	Introductions
5 minutes	Gathering Prayer
10 minutes	Overview of Eight-Session Program
20 minutes	Teaching 1: What Is Liturgy?
10 minutes	Break
20 minutes	Teaching 2: What Are Symbols?
10 minutes	Reflection: Entrance Song *through* Greeting
30 minutes	Prayer: Altar Prayer
15 minutes	Group Process
15 minutes	Intent: Entrance Song *through* Greeting

Resource Sheets

Recommended Reading

◊ Empereur, "The People Shout Amen—The Ministry of the Liturgical Assembly," *Worship: Exploring the Sacred.*

◊ *The Constitution on the Sacred Liturgy,* chapters 1 and 2.

◊ Kolodziej, "Typology of the Exodus—Passover," *Understanding the Mass,* 24.

Overview

This session is a time for making connections within the group and for laying a good foundation upon which the rest of your program will be built. There is a great deal of teaching in this session—perhaps more than in any other. It is important that your participants understand what liturgy and symbols are all about before you begin to address the specific parts of the liturgy. It is likely that many of them have had little formal education as adults in this area.

You cover the parts of the liturgy from the Entrance Song through the Greeting. The reflection for this session is short—five questions. This is the only week that a sharing time does not immediately follow; this week, we move right from reflection to prayer. Once the prayer is over and you have returned to your regular meeting place, sharing will begin. Because this is the first week, it might be best if people share in several small groups rather than one large one, although you will be the best judge of that. As we mentioned before, some people find large groups more intimidating; some find small groups that way, too. In addition to inviting people to share their reflections, you might ask if anyone would like to share his/her experience of the altar prayer.

If you choose to have general discussion rather than personal sharing, we have included some appropriate questions. However, we feel it is important for people to share reflections or their experiences of prayer this week so that they begin to get the feel for it. General discussion can come later; it works well in a classroom situation, but you are trying to weave this people into a praying community for the duration of this program. This is a different process, one that involves risk-taking on each person's part.

Your prayer this week focuses on the symbol of the altar/table. You will do the antiphonal readings taken from Scripture, incense the altar and then reverence it with a bow and a kiss.

Questionnaire

Before introductions begin, invite each person to fill out the questionnaire on page 42. This will help participants do a little focusing and it will help you get a sense of the group of people who have gathered together for this program.

As you prepare for Session 1, you might ponder or bring to prayer the following questions:

◊ What helps you feel initially comfortable in a group of people?

◊ What would help you feel committed to any new undertaking?

Introductions

Once people have completed the questionnaires, begin introductions. This first session is a critical time in the birth of your program, a time for introductions—introductions to one another and to the program itself. If you are working with a small group, chances are that many people already know each other. Nevertheless, it is still important to allow for introductions because the "knowing" that will evolve in this program is a different type of knowing—born of reflection, sharing and prayer—rather than a knowing that comes from being neighbors, serving on various committees together or having children on the same Little League team or in the same Girl Scout troop. Both types of knowing are necessary for a sense of wholeness.

The knowing that comes from reflection, sharing and prayer is generally deeper and more intimate, delicate, nuanced and confidential. It will take nurturing and care on your part to facilitate the birth of this type of knowing and strengthen this community who have gathered out of a desire to grow in their experience of liturgy, which expresses in part their relationship with the God who so loves them.

You may want to use a favorite "ice-breaker"; if not, simply go around the circle, inviting each person to give his/her name, perhaps a few pertinent things about him/herself, and why he/she is here.

Gathering Prayer

Introduction

For this first session, you will pray the Gathering Prayer, a simple responsorial prayer of thanksgiving and petition.

Outline

1. Distribute photocopies of the prayer to the entire group.
2. Ask for volunteers for R1 and R2.

Presenter Preparation

Your own preparation for prayer should include the following:

◊ Make copies of the Gathering Prayer, page 43.

Details

There are no additional details for this prayer.

You shall be called by a
new name
pronounced by the
mouth of the LORD....
And as a bridegroom
rejoices in his bride
so shall your God
rejoice in you.
— Isaiah 62:2,5

Overview of the Eight-Session Program

Take this time to explain to the participants the basic format of the program with its four major parts: reflection, group process, intent, and prayer. As you prepare for this explanation, you may want to refer to Part One: General Methodology, pages 12-24.

You may also want to explain how the sessions are divided—that you will be following the sequential order of liturgy. Explain how each session integrates the basic format of the program. As you prepare for this explanation, you may want to refer to the introduction to Part Two, page 28. Allow time for questions.

Teaching 1: What Is Liturgy?

The four main points to cover in this section are:

◊ Our eucharistic liturgy is a ritual.

◊ Our liturgy has a basic structure.

◊ Our eucharistic liturgy is rooted in the Jewish experience of Passover.

◊ We are all ministers by virtue of our baptism.

More than likely, you will need to do some reading and research for your twenty-minute presentation. There are many good resources out there; we recommend the following:

◊ Emminghaus, *Eucharist: Essence, Form, Celebration,* 6-21.

◊ Empereur, *Worship: Exploring the Sacred,* 11-31 (for your presentation on our shared ministry).

◊ Jorgensen, *Rekindling the Passion,* 35-46 (to begin your presentation on liturgy as ritual).

◊ Kolodziej, *Understanding the Mass,* 24 (to begin your presentation on liturgy rooted in the Jewish experience of Passover).

◊ Resource Sheet, "The Parts of the Mass," page 44 of this book, and the *General Instruction of the Roman Missal,* 24-57 (for the basic structure of the liturgy).

The people of God shout Amen not to their ordained ministers, but to themselves, as priests and celebrants of the worship of God.
— Empereur 19

What, then, is the unique message of the language of liturgical action? It tells us that we are whole humans, singly and together. It tells us that the bodies we are and the Body we are are holy.

— Ostdiek 29

Break

Teaching 2: What Are Symbols?

The two main points to cover in this section are:

◊ A definition of the symbolic nature of words, actions and objects

◊ A specific look at some of the words, actions and objects used in liturgy

Again, should you need resources upon which to base your presentation, we recommend the following:

◊ Fischer, *Signs, Words and Gestures.* This little book is a delightful collection of Fr. Balthasar's homilies that address liturgical words, actions and objects. Surprisingly, the section for children, pages 57-77, is particularly helpful for a specific look at these items.

◊ Jorgensen, *Rekindling the Passion*, 107-118 (for a definition of symbols).

◊ Ostdiek, *Catechesis for Liturgy*, 121-129, 137-142, 151-160 (these pages look specifically at liturgical action, objects and speech respectively).

◊ *Environment and Art in Catholic Worship,* 56-103 (for a specific look at words, actions and objects. While some of the information may seem obvious or overstated, reading through these points will give you a greater sense of the symbolic).

Reflection: Entrance Song *through* Greeting

Distribute the reflection sheets, photocopied from page 45, to each participant.

Altar Prayer

Introduction

This session's prayer focuses on the symbol of the altar. If done slowly and reverently, it should take you about half an hour. If you are holding your program within close proximity of an actual church building, then this prayer is best done in the building. If this is not possible, is it possible for you to establish a prayer area that includes some sort of make-shift altar? An altar of some sort is central to this prayer.

Outline

1. Process in silence, two by two, to the worship space.

2. In the center aisle of the church, in front of the sanctuary or altar area, remain in pairs and face each other. Pray the antiphonal reading.

3. Presenter incenses the altar.

4. Each person reverences the altar, after which he/she sits in a pew or returns to his/her regular seat, depending on your setup.

5. Provide a short period of silence once everyone is done reverencing the altar.

6. Silently process back to the space where the regular session will continue.

Presenter Preparation

Your own preparation for prayer should include the following:

◊ Prepare the censer or thurible that you will be using to incense the altar. Make sure you have matches handy (something we were often desperately looking for at the last minute) with which to light the incense.

◊ Make photocopies of the prayer sheet (page 43) for each person.

◊ Prepare the altar, including proper lighting.

Details

Explain how the reverencing is to be done: Make a deep bow in front of the altar, walk around to the other side of the altar (facing the worship space) and kiss the altar. Your explanation should include a physical demonstration of the reverencing and perhaps an invitation to everyone to practice. Gauge the group. Ask yourself if participants need to practice; if so, are they willing?

Introduction

Begin the prayer in your regular meeting space with an explanation that invites the participants to focus on the altar. Your invitation might be a paraphrase of the following:

As we begin to reflect on this most basic part of our experience of liturgy, how many of us are aware of the many levels of

> The prayers and kissing the altar had an impact—I experienced a connection with the Lord I didn't know I deserved.
> — A Participant

At the altar, the sacrifice of the cross is made present under sacramental signs. It is also the table of the Lord and the people of God are called together to share in it. The altar is, as well, the center of the thanksgiving that the eucharist accomplishes.
— GI 259

meaning that are beckoning to us through the altar? One of the early Vatican II documents, the *General Instruction of the Roman Missal*, accords the altar a central place in our worship. This position is solidly based on Scripture; there are many Jewish and Christian Scripture references to not only the altar but its very substance, which was traditionally stone. By prayerfully looking at some of these pieces of Scripture, we begin the journey into the heart of the symbolism of the altar and its stone. The altar gives us a physical place at which we gather; it embodies the presence of Christ among us and our own call to his priesthood; it draws us into the heart of our being where we discover our inner altar, the presence of Christ within us.

Antiphonal Reading

If you are the only presenter, ask for a second reader. Make sure that everyone has a copy of the prayer sheet. Invite the participants to process silently to your prayer/church space. Gather in a double line just in front of the sanctuary or temporary altar. Pause for several moments before you begin, drinking in the space and preparing your hearts for prayer.

Incensing the Altar

Once you finish the antiphonal reading, incense the altar. Be conscious of and generous with your action and the incense. (If you have never incensed before, ask someone to help you practice first.)

Reverencing the Altar

After you finish incensing, everyone, one by one, reverences the altar. As the presenter, model the reverencing first. Walk slowly into the sanctuary and stand in front of the altar. Do a deep, generous bow from the waist. (Genuflecting is generally reserved for when you are in front of the tabernacle.) Walk to the other side of the altar and gently kiss the center, where the stone lies under the altar cloth. A corporal (a small, square altar cloth) should be over that place. If you are in an actual church building, walk back into the nave of the church and sit in one of the first pews, waiting for everyone to finish.

Concluding Prayer

Once everyone has sat for a moment in silence, lead them back to your regular gathering space. If you are in a makeshift prayer space and there is no additional seating, your only option may be to return to your regular gathering space once a person has done the reverencing. This should be done in silence.

Group Process

For group process, you may have a group sharing, using the questions on the reflection sheet. Or you may have a group sharing that focuses on your prayer experience with the altar. Regarding that experience, you might ask the following questions:

◊ What was the overall experience like for you?

◊ What were you most aware of?

◊ What was most moving for you during the prayer?

◊ Having had this experience, do you think that you are or will be more aware of the altar as a symbol? Why? How?

If you prefer having a general discussion during this time, you may choose to focus on some general questions about the Mass, Mass attendance, etc., using questions similar to those in the questionnaire:

◊ Why do you go to Mass?

◊ What do you find most distracting when you are in church?

◊ What things you would like to see changed in the Mass? Why?

◊ What part of the Mass evokes the most feeling for you?

Intent:
Entrance Song *through* Greeting

Lead your discussion based on the intent sheet beginning on page 48.

This concludes Session 1.

LORD, I call to you;
  come quickly to help
  me;
  listen to my plea when
  I call.
Let my prayer be incense
  before you;
  my uplifted hands an
  evening sacrifice.
    — Psalm 141:1-2

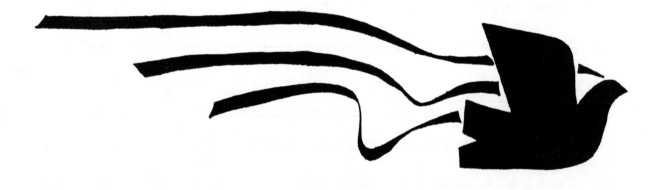

Session 1 Resource Sheets

Participant Questionnaire

Before you begin this program, it will be helpful for us (and we hope for you), if you would answer these few questions:

1. Why are you here and what would you like to receive from this program?

_____

_____

_____

2. Why do you go to Mass? What is the most important part of the Mass for you?

_____

_____

_____

3. What distracts you the most when you are in church?

_____

_____

_____

4. What part of the Mass, if any, is the hardest part for you to understand or to relate to? Why?

_____

_____

_____

5. What part of the Mass evokes the most feeling for you? Can you briefly describe the feeling?

_____

_____

_____

6. How did you come to sign up for this program (a friend, mailing, poster, etc.)?

_____

Gathering Prayer

Reader 1: Gentle God, you gather us as your people.
You love us and shape us and call us to be your beloved.

All: **Gentle God, you gather us as your people.**
You love us and shape us and call us to be your beloved.

Reader 2: Loving God, we thank you for calling us by name.
We thank you, too, for bringing us together for this program.
We ask you to help us recognize your presence here among us.

All: **Gentle God, you gather us as your people.**
You love us and shape us and call us to be your beloved.

Reader 1: Compassionate God, we ask you to help us be gentle
and loving toward one another as we begin this journey,
as we meet new people and encounter old friends.

All: **Gentle God, you gather us as your people.**
You love us and shape us and call us to be your beloved.

Reader 2: God of Wisdom, you are at once the flame and ember of our hearts.
As we gather together for this program,
may we be open to your knowledge.
May it be your wisdom that fuels the flame
and breathes upon the ember.

All: **Gentle God, you gather us as your people.**
You love us and shape us and call us to be your beloved.

Reader 1: God of Joy,
we thank you for mountains of laughter and valleys of tears.
May it be your joy that takes root in our hearts
as we journey together during the coming weeks.

All: **Gentle God, you gather us as your people.**
You love us and shape us and call us to be your beloved.

Reader 2: God of Light,
you transform the world of darkness into a world full of light.
You transform the world of broken dreams
into a world of hopeful promises.
May you transform us into a people who bear this light
to one another as Christ has borne it to us.

All: **Gentle God, you gather us as your people.**
You love us and shape us and call us to be your beloved.

The Parts of the Mass

(adapted from the General Instruction of the Roman Missal*)*

INTRODUCTORY RITES

> Entrance
>
> Veneration of the Altar and Greeting of the Congregation
>
> Penitential Rite
>
> Kyrie Eleison
>
> Gloria
>
> Opening Prayer or Collect

LITURGY OF THE WORD

> Scripture Readings
>
> Chants between the Readings (Responsorial Psalm)
>
> Homily
>
> Profession of Faith
>
> General Intercessions

LITURGY OF THE EUCHARIST[1]

> Preparation of the Gifts
>
> Eucharistic Prayer
>
> Communion Rite

CONCLUDING RITE

> Greeting and Blessing
>
> Dismissal

---

[1] For the individual elements of the Eucharistic Prayer and the Communion Rite, refer to GI 55a-h and 56 a-g.

Reflection: Entrance Song *through* Greeting

GATHERING THE ASSEMBLY (1)

To you, my God, I lift my soul, I trust in you; let me never come to shame. Do not let my enemies laugh at me. No one who waits for you is ever put to shame.

ENTRANCE SONG

After the people have assembled, the priest and the ministers go to the altar while the entrance song is being sung.(2)

When the priest comes to the altar, he makes the customary reverence(3) with the ministers, kisses(3) the altar and (if incense is used) incenses(3) it. Then, with the ministers, he goes to the chair.

GREETING

After the entrance song, the priest and the faithful remain standing and make the sign of the cross, as the priest says:

In the name of the Father, and of the Son, and of the Holy Spirit.(4)

The people answer:

Amen.

Then the priest, facing the people, extends his hands and greets all present:

The grace of our Lord Jesus Christ and the love of God and the fellowship of the Holy Spirit(5) be with you all.

The people answer:

C: And also with you.

(1) What do you do and how do you feel as you come into the church building and assemble for worship?

(2) Do you sing? If you do, what does the singing mean to you? How does it differ from speaking? Are you aware of others singing around you?

(3) If you are aware of these gestures of reverencing, kissing and incensing, what do they represent for you?

(4) What happens to you as you make the sign of the cross? How is it meaningful?

(5) What feelings do you have as you stand in fellowship with the Trinity and with each other?

Altar Prayer: An Antiphonal Reading

Reader 1:   Our altar is the Table of the Lord, the holy place
             where we come together to offer thanks and praise.

Reader 2:   I wash my hands in innocence,
                 and walk round your altar, LORD,
             Lifting my voice in thanks,
                 recounting all your wondrous deeds.
             LORD, I love the house where you dwell,
                 the tenting-place of your glory (Ps 26:6-8).

**All: Our altar is the Table of the Lord, the holy place
            where we come together to offer thanks and praise.**

Short pause for silent reflection

Reader 1:   Our altar is the holy place where our prayers
             rise like incense to you, O God.

Reader 2:   Another angel came and stood at the altar, holding a gold censer.
             He was given a great quantity of incense to offer, along with the
             prayers of all the holy ones, on the gold altar that was before the
             throne. The smoke of the incense along with the prayers of the
             holy ones went up before God from the hand of the angel (Rv
             8:3-4).

**All: Our altar is the holy place where our prayers
            rise like incense to you, O God.**

Short pause for silent reflection

Reader 1:   Our altar is the presence of Christ among us.

Reader 2:   Therefore, thus says the Lord GOD:
                 See, I am laying a stone in Zion, a stone that has
                     been tested,
             A precious cornerstone as a sure foundation;
                 he who puts his faith in it shall not be shaken
                     (Is 28:16).

All: Our altar is the presence of Christ among us.

Short pause for silent reflection

Reader 1:   At our altar, the sacrifice of the cross is made present
             in sacrament and grace.

Reader 2:   The stone the builders rejected
                 has become the cornerstone.
             By the LORD has this been done;
                 it is wonderful in our eyes (Ps 118:22-23).

Altar Prayer: An Antiphonal Reading (page 2)

All: **At our altar, the sacrifice of the cross is made present in sacrament and grace.**

Short pause for silent reflection

Reader 1: Our living altar calls us to be a holy priesthood and to share in the sacrifice of the Lord.

Reader 2: Come to [Jesus], a living stone, rejected by human beings but chosen and precious in the sight of God, and, like living stones, let yourselves be built into a spiritual house to be a holy priesthood to offer spiritual sacrifices acceptable to God through Jesus Christ (1 Pt 2:4-5).

All: **Our living altar calls us to be a holy priesthood and to share in the sacrifice of the Lord.**

Short pause for silent reflection

Reader 1: At our altar, God feeds us and sends us forth to be Christ for one another.

Reader 2: But you are "a chosen race, a royal priesthood, a holy nation, a people of his own, so that you may announce the praises" of him who called you out of darkness into his wonderful light.

Once you were "no people"
   but now you are God's people;
you "had not received mercy"
   but now you have received mercy (1 Pt 2:9-10).

All: **At our altar, God feeds us and sends us forth to be Christ for one another.**

Short pause for silent reflection

Intent: Entrance Song *through* Greeting

INTRODUCTORY RITES(1)

ENTRANCE ANTIPHON

To you, my God, I lift my soul, I trust in you; let me never come to shame. Do not let my enemies laugh at me. No one who waits for you is ever put to shame.(2)

ENTRANCE SONG(3)

After the people have assembled, the priest and the ministers go to the altar while the entrance song is being sung.

(1) The Introductory Rites include the Entrance Song or Antiphon, the Greeting, the Penitential Rite or the Rite of Blessing, Kyrie, Gloria, and the Opening Prayer; these introduce the Liturgy of the Word and serve to connect us with each other—we are one. They allow us to properly dispose ourselves to listening to the Word of God and to celebrating the Eucharist worthily. What these rites say to us is, "Let us begin, let us become aware of one another, let us prepare ourselves for worship."

(2) Each liturgy has its own Entrance Antiphon, which is usually a psalm of praise. This particular antiphon is prayed on the First Sunday of Advent and is taken from Psalm 25:1-3. The focus on waiting complements the Advent mood of anticipation; the Entrance Antiphon generally reflects the liturgical season or feast. The Entrance Antiphon is recited only if there is no Entrance Song.

(3) "The purpose of [the Entrance Song] is to open the celebration, intensify the unity of the gathered people, lead their thoughts to the mystery of the season or feast, and accompany the procession of priest and ministers" (GI 25). The song is so important to the celebration that we rarely begin liturgy without it. The song is often based on the Entrance Antiphon. The deeper breathing needed to sing and the effort expended in the process draw the body and the soul together.

The procession of the priest and the ministers of the day calls the people to focus on one event, thereby further unifying us as all our attention is drawn to the procession. With this focus, we begin the process of deepening our awareness of unity that culminates with the Eucharist.

Intent: Entrance Song through Greeting (page 2)

When the priest comes to the altar, he makes the customary reverence(4) with the ministers, kisses(4) the altar and (if incense is used) incenses(4) it. Then, with the ministers, he goes to the chair.

GREETING

After the entrance song, the priest and the faithful remain standing and make the sign of the cross, as the priest says:

In the name of the Father, and of the Son, and of the Holy Spirit(5).

The people answer:

Amen.

Then the priest, facing the people, extends his hands and greets all present:

The grace of our Lord Jesus Christ and the love of God and the fellowship of the Holy Spirit be with you all(6).

The people answer:

And also with you.

(4) The reverencing at the altar is done because the altar symbolizes "Jesus Christ as well as the whole Christian community, the living stones from which the Lord Jesus builds the Church's altar" (Manly and Reinhard 244). It is done by either genuflecting or bowing. Genuflection is reserved for the presence of the Eucharist. The kiss symbolizes the desired or achieved union with Jesus. Incense is used as a sign of honor. It also symbolizes and embodies our hope that our prayers will rise to God in the same way that incense rises.

(5) The first part of the Greeting is the sign of the cross. It is an act of self-blessing before prayer. The forehead symbolizes understanding; the breast, heart and feelings; shoulder to shoulder, the arms and hands with which we work and bear fruit. The sign of the cross originates in Matthew 28:19: "Go, therefore, and make disciples of all the nations, baptizing them in the name of the Father, and of the Son, and of the holy Spirit...." This is the baptismal command of Jesus. It connects us to our own baptism and also acknowledges our understanding of God as three persons. The sign of the cross has also come to be a "badge of membership of his Body" (Manly and Reinhard 245). It is an expression of faith, prayer, devotion and willingness to participate in the liturgy actively. It is our statement that salvation comes to us through the cross.

(6) The second part of the Greeting firmly establishes the relationship between the priest and the people. The desire for grace is a reciprocal one—the priest prays it for the people, and the people pray it for the priest. This greeting "declares to the assembled community that the Lord is present. This greeting and the congregation's response express the mystery of the gathered Church" (GI 28). This particular greeting is the first of three options in the Sacramentary and the only one that is explicitly trinitarian.

Session 2:
Penitential Rite *through* Opening Prayer

As worshiping assembly, we celebrate God's mercy.

Schedule

Time	Description
5 minutes	Gathering Prayer
10 minutes	Teaching 1: A Theology of Blessing and Our Call to General Priesthood
30 minutes	Prayer: Blessing of Water and Sprinkling Rite
10 minutes	Group Process 1
20 minutes	Reflection: Penitential Rite *through* Opening Prayer
5 minutes	Break
20 minutes	Group Process 2
20 minutes	Intent: Penitential Rite *through* Opening Prayer
30 minutes	Teaching 2: Praying with Scripture

Resource Sheets

Recommended Reading

◊ Stauffer, "The Why of Worship," *Worship* 65 (January 1989): 45-49.

Overview

This session is a time for putting into practice the general ministry of all the baptized. Much has been written about this ministry, but there is limited opportunity to use this gift in its fullness unless a person is in professional ministry. On a parish level, you will find many who are unfamiliar with the concept.

During this session, you introduce the Gathering Prayer, which will remain the same for all the sessions. It is short and designed to help each person create contemplative space within the group and find it within themselves. See the Gathering Prayer section for a step-by-step description of this prayer.

In this session, you cover the parts of the liturgy from the Penitential Rite through the Opening Prayer. You begin with a short teaching on the theology of blessing and general ministry, building upon the points made during the last session about our call to ministry. For information about these parts of the Mass, consider the following resources:

◊ Emminghaus, *Eucharist: Essence, Form, Celebration*, 116-133.

◊ Johnson, *Word & Eucharist Handbook*, 19-26.

◊ General Instruction of the Roman Missal, 29-32, 87-88.

◊ *Music in Catholic Worship*, 65-66.

◊ Baldovin, "Kyrie Eleison and the Entrance Rite of the Roman Eucharist," *Worship: City, Church and Renewal*, 135-150.

The session's prayer is a Rite of Blessing and Sprinkling, which is one of the options available in the Penitential Rite. You have about ten minutes to process this prayer immediately after its conclusion.

The reflection for this session is rather long—eleven questions. Draw attention to five or six questions as the most important ones to give participants some sense of timing and priority. We recommend numbers 4, 6, 7, 9, and 10.

You conclude this session with a presentation on how to pray with Scripture. This anticipates and prepares everyone for the next session, which looks at the Liturgy of the Word. At the end of the presentation, ask for readers for the Proclamation of the Word, which you will celebrate during the next session. What readings should you pick? We recommend using the readings for the Sunday preceding your third session. If you are singing the psalm, choose a setting that is familiar to your group, perhaps the common psalm your community has been using for the particular liturgical season you are currently in.

Presenter's Reflection Questions

As you prepare for Session 2, you might ponder or bring to prayer the following questions:

◊ What is your sense of belonging to the "royal priesthood of believers"?

◊ How might you best help someone recognize his/her call to this priesthood?

◊ What is your own experience of water as a symbol?

Coming together as
  God's family,
with confidence let us
  ask the Father's
  forgiveness,
for he is full of gentleness
  and compassion.
    — Penitential Rite B

We assemble for worship
on Sundays to stand in
God's presence—and
actually to encounter
God in the Face of Jesus
Christ. Gathered to hear
the gospel of love and
freedom and assembled
around the altar to feast
on the food of eternal
life, we meet God in a
profound and wonderful
way.
    — Stauffer 46

Gathering Prayer

Introduction

The regular gathering prayer is, in part, an abbreviated form of centering. We find it a very helpful way to gather for the evening. It takes between five and seven minutes. There are four aspects to this opening prayer:

◊ To "center" on the here and now through letting go of tensions/concerns/preoccupations.

◊ To become more aware of God's presence among and within your group.

◊ To give thanks.

◊ To ask God's blessing and assistance for all that you will do during this session.

Outline

1. Gather everyone into the circle.

2. Light the candle.

3. Guide the participants through the prayer.

Presenter Preparation

Your own preparation for prayer should include the following:

◊ Prepare your prayer space. For ideas, refer to "Creating Your Session Space" in the Introduction, page 3.

◊ Make sure you have a candle and matches.

◊ Consider writing out the exact words you will say, based on the details below.

Details

Pray the Gathering Prayer slowly, keeping your voice nicely modulated and even.

1. Gather everyone into the circle.

2. Begin by lighting the candle on the table in the middle of the circle in a mindful, prayerful way.[1] The lighting of the candle is the beginning of your prayer.

3. Explain that you will be taking the participants through a number of steps and that if they are unable to proceed to the next step for whatever reason, they may honor their own needs and space.

---

[1] See the chapter titled "Prayer" for a description of prayerfulness and mindfulness.

4. Invite participants to take three or four deep breaths, drawing the air in slowly and expelling it slowly, being as fully aware as possible of both actions.

5. Invite participants to do a "body survey." Where are they feeling tension? We often carry tension in our bodies; our shoulders, jaw, face, and hands are common places. Ask if they can relax some of those parts, even just a little bit.

6. Invite participants to focus their attention on the candle, reminding them that it is the symbol of God's presence within your group. Pause for a moment.

7. Invite participants to breathe in the light of the candle, allowing it to fill their inner space completely. Pause for a moment.

8. Invite participants to breathe out their tensions, problems, darkness and to let the light completely fill them. Pause for a moment.

9. Invite participants to give thanks silently in a way that is most comfortable for them: thanks to our God who gathers us here in this time and space; thanks to our God for all that God gives us; thanks to our God who sustains us; thanks to our God who so loves us.

10. Conclude by addressing God in a form that is familiar to you. You may ask participants to silently address God in their own words as well. Then ask God to bless all that you are about in this time, to open your ears to all that God desires you to hear, to open your minds and hearts to all that God desires you to know, to open your mouths to speak all that God desires you to say.

Teaching 1: A Theology of Blessing and Our Call to General Priesthood

The three main points to cover in this section are:

◊ Review the ministry of the baptized.

◊ Review the symbolic nature of words, actions, and objects, focusing on water in particular.

◊ Discuss the nature and components of blessing.

You might want to do some reading and research for your ten-minute presentation, although there is not enough time to delve into great detail on any one point. Your primary goal here is to help people feel comfortable with the prayer of blessing they will confer on the water and the sprinkling they will do upon each other. Keep this in mind

But you are "a chosen race, a royal priesthood, a holy nation, a people of (God's) own, so that you may announce the praises" of him who called you out of darkness into his wonderful light.
— 1 Peter 2:9

The liturgical assembly, as presented, is Church, and as Church is servant to the world. It has a commitment to be sign, witness, and instrument of the reign of God.

— EACW 38

as you prepare for this teaching. Of the many good resources out there, we recommend the following:

◊ Empereur, *Worship: Exploring the Sacred*, 11-31 (for ministry)

◊ Powers, "Ministry," especially the section entitled "Vatican II," 836-837 (for ministry)

◊ Jorgensen, *Rekindling the Passion*, 107-118 (for symbols)

To aid in your discussion of blessing, draw upon the following:

Scriptural References to "Blessing"

In the bible, the word "blessing" has several different meanings, depending on the people and circumstances involved. A blessing may make something holy, may be a hymn of praise, or may be a wish for happiness and well being. You may want to look at passages from Scripture that mention "blessing": Genesis 12:2-3; Psalm 103:1-5,19-23; Daniel 3:20-88; Mark 10:13-16; Acts 3:25-26. Portions of these are reprinted below.

Types of Blessings

Blessings are conferred by God upon God's people. When God blesses God's people, the blessing is given in the form of material or spiritual benefits, and it often embraces both the present and the future. We see this type of blessing in Genesis 12:2-3:

> I will make of you a great nation and I will bless you; I will make your name great, so that you will be a blessing. I will bless those who bless you and curse those who curse you. All the communities of the earth shall find blessing in you.

When the blessing includes a future time, the blessing becomes a promise as well. Throughout Scripture, we see this particular type of blessing conferred and repeated. In the Acts of the Apostles (3:25-26), Peter addresses the crowd, reminding them once again of God's blessing and promise:

> You are the children of the prophets and of the covenant that God made with your ancestors when he said to Abraham, "In your offspring all the families of the earth shall be blessed." For you first, God raised up his servant and sent him to bless you by turning each of you from your evil ways.

Blessings are also conferred by God's people upon God. The blessing in this case has a different meaning. When the people bless God, the blessing is a form of praise. Here are two good examples of this:

> Bless the LORD, O my soul;
> and all my being, bless his holy name.

Bless the LORD, O my soul,
  and forget not all his benefits;... (Ps 103:1-2).

Bless the Lord, all you works of the Lord,
  praise and exalt him above all forever (Dn 3:57).

The litany in Daniel continues for over thirty verses. Our eucharistic prayers have roots in the Jewish blessing prayer, the *berakah*. The blessing in this case is an eloquent and highly ritualized form of praise and thanksgiving for all God has given us.

Blessings are also conferred by people upon other people and by people upon objects. The blessing by people upon other people is often in the form of wishing them well. The blessing by people upon objects is usually done to consecrate these objects to God; this act of consecration makes these people and objects more holy in the eyes of the community. When we bless the water, we are asking the Spirit to come and make this water holy.

Elements of Blessings by People upon People or Objects

Blessings conferred by people upon other people and upon objects usually contain five elements. The elements listed here are adapted from *The Blessing* by Gary Smalley and John Trent, PhD.

The first element is touch. The touch is not always physical. When we extend our hands over a person or object, the touch is symbolic because the gesture (not the touch itself) conveys the blessing. During the liturgy, the priest uses this gesture on several different occasions. When we bless the water, we will do this.

Blessings usually contain a spoken message. The Scriptural blessings cited above contain such a message. When we bless the water, we will speak words that invite God to bless the water through the Spirit, using our hands as the instrument of the blessing.

Blessings attach a high value to the person/object being blessed. Once the water is blessed, it has a higher value for us as a community. After the community concludes the Sprinkling Rite, the water retains its higher value.

A blessing is both a now and future event. When the blessing becomes a future event, it is a promise. The blessing of water happens now, but through the blessing it also carries a promise: "May this water become an instrument of your cleansing and forgiveness." The water is a symbol of God's forgiveness now and in the future.

Blessings also contain the element of active commitment. When we invite God to confer a blessing upon the water, we invite God to "bind us to one another in faith-filled love and heartfelt service." God

---

Consequently, those who have faith are blessed along with Abraham who had faith.
— Galatians 3:9

Everything growing from
  the earth,
  bless the Lord;....
You springs,
  bless the Lord;....
Seas and rivers,
  bless the Lord;....
You dolphins and all
  water creatures,
  bless the Lord,....
— Daniel 3:76-79

desires our cooperation, and this particular blessing implies a willingness and commitment on our part to love and serve.

Prayer: Blessing of Water and Sprinkling Rite

Introduction

This week's prayer is a blessing of water and sprinkling rite. This prayer works within your regular session space; make sure you have a table that is large enough to hold a medium-sized (three-quart) bowl and a small pine bough, branch or leaf. You could use your regular table, but move it to the front of the room so that there is enough room to have a sense of procession to the table.

Outline

1. Begin by singing the song "Sing of a Blessing" by Miriam Therese Winter.
2. Bless the water.
3. In pairs, sprinkle water upon one another.
4. Return to chairs.
5. Recite the Responsorial Prayer.
6. Follow with a short period of silence.
7. Conclude with group process that looks at the prayer experience.

Presenter Preparation

Your own preparation for prayer should include the following:

◊ Place on the table a medium-sized bowl (preferably clear glass) and a small pine bough, branch or large leaf that will hold droplets of water.

◊ Prepare a single copy in large print of the words that accompany the Sprinkling Rite:

I will sprinkle clean water upon you to cleanse you from all your impurities [says the Lord GOD] (Ez 36:25).

◊ Photocopy the prayer sheets, pages 66-67.

Details

You may choose to explain the prayer or you may choose to rely on modeling. If you choose modeling, make sure you are at the head of the line. We recommend, however, at this point in the program that

What was the most moving part of the program for you and why?

The blessing of the water and each other. I was very moved...to be empowered to participate in God-giving grace.

— A Participant

you give a brief explanation; the modeling can come later, when people are more familiar with the program and its process.

The song has a simple melody that is done in responsorial style with a cantor. You might want to sing along with the tape as, in this particular case, it works quite well.

When you bless the water, hold the bowl up or invite someone to hold it. Invite everyone to extend one hand over the bowl (you will be in your regular circle at this time, so each person's hand will not be physically over the bowl) as you pray the blessing together.

Next, proceed with the Rite of Sprinkling. If your physical space allows, process in twos to the table at the front of the room. Invite two people to carry the pine bough, branch or leaf and the bowl of water. The words from Ezekiel should already be on the table, preferably encased in some sort of plastic (laminated, covered with clear contact paper, or wrapped in a plastic bag folded neatly).

Form a line of pairs in front of the table. Once the first two people have placed the bowl and "sprinkler" on the table and returned to their places in line, you are ready to begin the sprinkling. The first pair approaches the table. One person takes the "sprinkler," dips it in water and sprinkles it upon the other, speaking the words of Ezekiel. Then they reverse the process. When they are done, they return silently to their regular seats in the circle.

Group Process 1

This group process time is very short—ten minutes. Gauge the group; they might not need the time to process this prayer or it may be too soon for them to say anything (especially if they were very moved). Because it may be a relatively new experience for many of them ("Who, me? Bless water? Sprinkle someone else?"), they may be bursting at the seams to talk about it. You may just need to invite comment or you might feel more comfortable starting with some questions regarding that experience:

◊ What was the overall experience like for you?

◊ What were you most aware of?

◊ What was most moving for you during the prayer?

◊ Were there awkward or uncomfortable moments for you? What caused them?

◊ How or what are you feeling right now?

To bless whatever there is, and for no other reason but simply because it is—that is our raison d'être, that is what we are made for as human beings.
— Steindl-Rast 81

May the axe be far
  away from you;
May the fire be far away
  from you;
May there be rain
  without storm;
Lord of Trees, may you
  be blessed;
Lord of Trees, may I be
  blessed.
— "Hindu Prayer,"
Earth Prayers 361

Reflection: Penitential Rite *through* Opening Prayer

Distribute the reflection sheets, photocopied from pages 68-70, to each participant.

Break

Group Process 2

We recommend that you stay with the reflection questions instead of doing a general discussion. If you have stated ahead of time which are the most important questions (numbers 4, 6, 7, 9, and 10), begin with those. Another way you might work with this particular group process (because there are so many reflection questions) is to ask the group which was the easiest question for them to answer and why; which was the most difficult and why.

Intent: Penitential Rite *through* Opening Prayer

Lead your discussion based on the intent sheet beginning on page 71.

Teaching 2: Praying with Scripture

Then (Jesus) opened their minds to understand the scriptures.
— Luke 24:45

Rather than list resources or give you main points to cover in this second teaching, let's look at three methods of praying with scripture. During the liturgy itself, there is not enough time for extensive praying with the Scriptures, but you can guide people into entering the Scripture so that it comes alive for them by using any of these methods. Once the Scripture has become more than words for them, they can go back to it in prayer during the remainder of the day, as they go about daily tasks (like washing dishes or mowing the lawn) or set aside a quiet time for reflection.

Method 1: Finding the Main Point of the Scripture

With this method, you listen to the Scripture being proclaimed. As you listen, ask yourself, "What seems to be the main point or lesson in this scripture?" You do not need Scripture commentaries or exegesis to do this because what you are looking for is the personal point, the point in the Scripture that seems to be speaking to you right now. For example, in the cure of the man born blind (Mk 8:22-26), perhaps what you most clearly hear or what touches you the most is the physical healing of this man.

Once you have a sense of the main point, then you can ask a second question, "How does the physical healing of this man apply to my life?" At this point, you move into the symbolic level (unless, of course, you were born blind and were cured; there would then be a literal correlation).

To find the main point for your life, look for ways that you have been blind—perhaps you did not see the pain in your own life last year that was caused by being laid off and you pretended that everything was OK. Remember how your pain and anger came out in strange ways and at unexpected times? Or perhaps you did not see the difficult time your mother was having with your father, who had been recently confined to a wheelchair. Maybe you distanced yourself and pretended you were too busy to help out in any way.

And then recall how, suddenly, you saw these things and could then begin to deal with them! You had been blind to this area of your life and now you could see. Remember the surprise brought about by your initial recognition of the blind spot; remember the guilt at not having seen before; remember God's forgiveness of you even as the words "I'm sorry" were on your lips; remember your forgiveness of self that finally came several months later. God has, indeed, been alive in your life.

Or rather than placing the point of the Scripture in the past, you might ask yourself, "In what ways am I being blind right now?" This is the riskier approach, but also the one that will bring the most healing and growth. Both ways of approaching Scripture—reflecting on the past and looking at the present—are equally valid and needed.

Method 2: Entering the Scene

This method invites you to actually enter a Scripture passage through your imagination. A good Scripture passage to begin with is the story of the loaves and the fishes (Lk 9:10-17). First, picture the scene in your mind. Imagine not only what you can see but also what you can smell, hear, taste and touch. Second, enter the scene. Do not control your point of entry; allow the Spirit to guide you into the picture you have drawn in your head. Are you one of the crowd? Are you one of the disciples? Are you Jesus? Are you the loaf of bread or one of the fish?

This is a fairly creative method of responding to a reading (it is commonly called guided imagery; some may be less generous and call it far-fetched or way-out). It allows you to actually experience in some way what is happening in that particular reading. Try to

"Were not our hearts burning (within us) while (Jesus) spoke to us on the way and opened the scriptures to us?"
— Luke 24:32

...the Scriptures are the living waters from which all who seek life and salvation must drink.
— LI 5

stay with the experience once you have been sent forth from the liturgical celebration. Ask yourself questions like, "What was it like to be a disciple? one of the crowd? the loaf of bread? the fish?" Pose the question, "What is God saying to me in the experience?"

Method 3: Responding to the Reading from Your Heart

In this method, listen to the entire reading. Then make one statement from your heart as a response to the reading. This statement needs to be as spontaneous as you can possibly allow it to be. Let's look at how this method might work:

Reading II

A reading from the letter of Paul to the Romans (13:11-14)

The time has come, our salvation is near.

[Y]ou know the time;[1] it is the hour now for you to awake from sleep. For our salvation is nearer now than when we first believed; the night is advanced, the day is at hand.[2] Let us then throw off the works of darkness [and] put on the armor of light; let us conduct ourselves properly as in the day,[3] not in orgies and drunkenness, not in promiscuity and licentiousness, not in rivalry and jealousy. But put on the Lord Jesus Christ,[4] and make no provision for the desires of the flesh.

L: The Word of the Lord.

C: Thanks be to God.

Can these words become more than words for you? What are some of the possible personal responses that you can make in your heart to this reading? Can you begin to hear any of the words of this reading in your heart? Can you then speak your response to those words from that place in your heart where you have heard this Word? This response need not be sophisticated, theologically correct, nor carefully worded. It is a feeling response from your heart.

Let's look at four possible responses, which are based on a method found in *The Art of Praying Liturgy* by Gregory Manly and Anneliese Reinhard (139-145). The numbers of the responses correspond with the numbers found in the Scripture passage.

1. I am greatly saddened by the times we are living in.

2. I look forward to your daylight, dear Lord!

3. It is so hard for me to live honorably. Help me this day.

4. I welcome you into my heart with great joy!

To honor the response of your heart to the Word as it is proclaimed during the liturgy, you could pay attention to this response through-

---

(The faithful) must...be the bearers of (God's) word in the Church and in the world, at least by the witness of their way of life

—LI 7

When God shares (God's) word with us, (God) awaits our response, that is, our listening and our adoring "in Spirit and in truth (John 4:23)."

— LI 6

out your day or you could bring your response into your prayer life. Either of these options could lead you into a deeper response or a deeper or new commitment that springs from this Scripture. Let's see what could happen (again, the numbers correspond to the Scripture phrases and the initial responses above).

1. You might think of some country which is experiencing political or economic upheaval and pray for the people who are suffering as a result. If you are deeply touched, you might think about another level of commitment—a letter to your congressperson about our military expenditures, etc.

2. You may just allow that image of Jesus' light to begin to expand and fill your entire being to the extent that it really does bring you increased peace throughout your day.

3. You may find yourself reflecting on some issue of conscience that has been really bothering you. Your initial response about how hard it is may open you to heartfelt repentance about something this day.

4. As in response 2, this sense of "putting on the Lord Jesus Christ" may fill you with an inner contentment and peace for the entire day if you allow yourself to be open to it.

Again, you may have other methods of responding to Scripture. These ideas give you a basis for your half-hour presentation. You may choose to present only one method, explain it and then give a demonstration. Or you may briefly explain all three.

Before you dismiss the group, do not forget to ask for volunteers to proclaim the Word for the third session. If you have cantors or music ministers, you may also ask for a volunteer to sing the psalm.

This concludes Session 2.

In the word of God the divine covenant is announced.

— LI 10

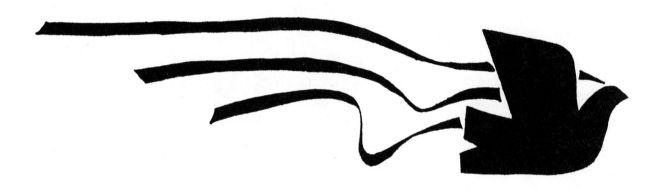

Session 2 Resource Sheets

Prayer: Blessing of Water and Sprinkling Rite

All join in "Sing of a Blessing" by Miriam Therese Winter:

Verse 1: Sing we, sing of a blessing. Sing we, sing of a blessing.
Sing we, sing of a blessing. Sing we, sing of a blessing.
A blessing of love. A blessing of love.
A blessing of mercy. A blessing of mercy.

Chorus: Love will increase, love will increase
a blessing of peace, a blessing of peace.

Verse 2: Pray now, pray for a blessing. Pray now, pray for a blessing.
Pray now, pray for a blessing. Pray now, pray for a blessing.
A blessing of joy. A blessing of joy.
A blessing of justice. A blessing of justice.

Verse 3: Share now, share in a blessing. Share now, share in a blessing.
Share now, share in a blessing. Share now, share in a blessing.
A blessing of hope. A blessing of hope.
A blessing of courage. A blessing of courage.

Verse 4: Live live, live as a blessing. Live live, live as a blessing.
Live live, live as a blessing. Live live, live as a blessing.
A blessing within. A blessing within.
A blessing among us. A blessing among us.

Verse 5: Send forth, send forth a blessing. Send forth, send forth a blessing.
Send forth, send forth a blessing. Send forth, send forth a blessing.
A blessing to all. A blessing to all.
Now and forever. Now and forever.

Blessing the Water

All pray together with hands outstretched:

Oh, God, through the breath of your Spirit,
bless this water we hold before you.
May this water become an instrument
of your cleansing and forgiveness.
Stir up your Spirit within us and bind us to one another
in faith-filled love and heartfelt service.
We ask this through Jesus Christ our Lord. Amen.

Rite of Sprinkling

Approach each side of the table in pairs. After dipping your pine bough, branch, or leaf into the
holy water, sprinkle each other and pray the following words from Ezekiel:

I will sprinkle clean water upon you
to cleanse you from all your impurities [says the Lord GOD].

Prayer: Blessing of Water and Sprinkling Rite (page 2)

Responsorial Prayer (based on Galatians 5)

Reader 1:   Holy Spirit,
            you lead us to love one another in the way Jesus has first loved us.

All: Bless us, Holy Spirit, giver of Love.

Reader 2:   Holy Spirit,
            in your presence we come to know joy that will never end.

All: Bless us, Holy Spirit, giver of Joy.

Reader 1:   Holy Spirit, you gift us with patience as we grow,
            as we struggle, and as we try to live together in community.

All: Bless us, Holy Spirit, giver of Patience.

Reader 2:   Holy Spirit, you are kind to us.
            Teach us to be kind to ourselves and to one another.

All: Bless us, Holy Spirit, giver of Kindness.

Reader 1:   Holy Spirit, you are generous in your presence with us
            and generous in responding to our needs.
            Teach us to be generous.

All: Bless us, Holy Spirit, giver of Generosity.

Reader 2:   Holy Spirit, you reveal for us the faithfulness of our God.
            Draw us to live more faithfully with you.

All: Bless us, Holy Spirit, giver of Faithfulness.

Reader 1:   Holy Spirit, you come to us in a gentle, whispering breeze.
            Teach us to be gentle with ourselves and with one another.

All: Bless us, Holy Spirit, giver of Gentleness.

Reader 2:   Holy Spirit, you call us to exercise self-control.
            Continue to be our guide as we seek to stand before you
            in holiness and virtue.

All: Bless us, Holy Spirit, giver of Self-Control.

Reflection: Penitential Rite *through* Opening Prayer

RITE OF BLESSING
AND SPRINKLING HOLY WATER

When this rite is celebrated it takes the place of the penitential rite at the beginning of Mass. The Kyrie is also omitted.

After greeting the people, the priest remains standing at his chair. A vessel containing the water to be blessed is placed before him. Facing the people, he invites them to pray, using these or similar words:

Dear friends,
this water will be used
to remind us of our baptism.
Let us ask God to bless it,
and to keep us faithful
to the Spirit(1) he has given us.

After a brief silence, he joins his hands and continues:

God our Father,
your gift of water
brings life and freshness to the earth;
it washes away our sins
and brings us eternal life.

We ask you now
to bless ✠ this water,
and to give us your protection on this day
which you have made your own.
Renew the living spring of your life within us
and protect us in spirit and body(2),
that we may be free from sin
and come into your presence
to receive your gift of salvation.

We ask this through Christ our Lord.

Taking the sprinkler, the priest sprinkles himself and his ministers, then the rest of the clergy and people. He may move through the church for the sprinkling of the people(3). Meanwhile, an antiphon or another appropriate song is sung.

When he returns to his place and the song is finished, the priest faces the people and, with joined hands, says:

(1) How are you faithful to the Spirit?

(2) What feelings does this phrase evoke in you?

(3) What does the Sprinkling Rite mean to you?

Reflection: Penitential Rite through Opening Prayer (page 2)

May almighty God cleanse us of our sins(4),
and through the eucharist we celebrate
make us worthy(5) to sit at his table
in his heavenly kingdom.

The people answer:

Amen.

PENITENTIAL RITE

*After the introduction to the day's Mass, the
priest invites the people to recall their sins and
to repent of them in silence. He may use these
or similar words:*

Coming together as God's family,
with confidence let us ask the Father's
    forgiveness,
for he is full of gentleness and compassion.

A pause for silent reflection follows.

After the silence...all say:

I confess(6) to almighty God,
and to you, my brothers and sisters,
that I have sinned through my own fault

They strike their breast

in my thoughts and in my words,
in what I have done,
and in what I have failed to do;
and I ask blessed Mary, ever virgin,
all the angels and saints,
and you, my brothers and sisters,
to pray for me(7) to the Lord our God.

The priest says the absolution:

May almighty God have mercy on us,
forgive us our sins,
and bring us to everlasting life.(8)

The people answer:

Amen.

KYRIE

V. Lord, have mercy.
R. Lord, have mercy.(9)
V. Christ, have mercy.
R. Christ, have mercy.
V. Lord, have mercy.
R. Lord, have mercy.

(4) How do you feel when God cleanses you of
your sin?

(5) What is it like for you to be made worthy?

(6) What does it mean for you to confess?

(7) What are you asking these people to pray for
and why do you ask them?

(8) What does this petition mean to you?

(9) How do you feel when you ask for mercy?

Reflection: Penitential Rite through Opening Prayer (page 3)

GLORIA

Glory to God in the highest,
    and peace to his people on earth.

Lord God, heavenly King,
almighty God and Father,
    we worship you, we give you thanks,
    we praise you for your glory.(10)

Lord Jesus Christ, only Son of the Father,
Lord God, Lamb of God,
you take away the sin of the world:
    have mercy on us;
you are seated at the right hand of the Father:
    receive our prayer.

For you alone are the Holy One,
you alone are the Lord,
you alone are the Most High,
    Jesus Christ,
    with the Holy Spirit,
    in the glory of God the Father. Amen.

OPENING PRAYER

*Afterwards the priest, with hands joined, sings
or says:*

Let us pray
    [in Advent time
    with longing(11) and waiting(11)
    for the coming of the Lord].

Priest and people pray silently for a while.

*Then the priest extends his hands and sings
or says the opening prayer:*

Father in heaven,
our hearts desire(11) the warmth of your love
and our minds are searching(11) for the light
    of your Word.

Increase our longing(11) for Christ our Savior
and give us the strength to grow in love,
that the dawn of his coming
may find us rejoicing(11) in his presence
and welcoming(11) the light of his truth.

We ask this in the name of Jesus the Lord.

The people respond:

Amen.

(10) What moves you to worship, thank and praise God?

(11) Of all these feelings—longing, waiting, desiring, searching, rejoicing, and welcoming—which one speaks the most strongly to you and why?

Eucharist! © 1994 Resource Publications, Inc. All rights reserved.

Intent: Penitential Rite *through* Opening Prayer

RITE OF BLESSING
AND SPRINKLING HOLY WATER(1)

When this rite is celebrated it takes the place of the penitential rite at the beginning of Mass. The Kyrie is also omitted.

After greeting the people, the priest remains standing at his chair. A vessel containing the water to be blessed is placed before him. Facing the people, he invites them to pray, using these or similar words:

Dear friends,
this water will be used
to remind us of our baptism.
Let us ask God to bless it,
and to keep us faithful
to the Spirit he has given us.

After a brief silence, he joins his hands and continues:(2)

God our Father,
your gift of water
brings life and freshness to the earth;
it washes away our sins
and brings us eternal life.

We ask you now
to bless ✠(3) this water,
and to give us your protection on this day
which you have made your own.
Renew the living spring of your life within us
and protect us in spirit and body,
that we may be free from sin
and come into your presence
to receive your gift of salvation.

We ask this through Christ our Lord.

Taking the sprinkler, the priest sprinkles himself and his ministers, then the rest of the clergy and people. He may move through the church for the sprinkling of the people.

Meanwhile, an antiphon or another appropriate song is sung.

When he returns to his place and the song is finished, the priest faces the people and, with joined hands, says:

(1) The Rite of Blessing and Sprinkling Holy Water can be used during all Sunday Masses. If it is used, the Penitential Rite and the Kyrie are omitted. The Rite reminds us of our baptism—it is a call to renew our baptism. This rite became popular during the Middle Ages, when it was referred to as the "Asperges procession." "Asperges" is a Latin word meaning "thou shalt sprinkle"; it is used in the ninth verse of Psalm 51: "Cleanse me with hyssop, that I may be pure."

(2) This blessing of the water is one of three that may be used. Following the blessing, the priest may also mix salt into the water.

(3) This sign, ✠, indicates the places in the liturgy where the priest makes the sign of the cross as part of the blessing. The sign appears in four places: the blessing of the water, the blessing of the salt (optional), the first epiclesis of the Eucharistic Prayer (Eucharistic Prayer I is the exception), and the blessing given during the Concluding Rite.

Intent: Penitential Rite through Opening Prayer (page 2)

May almighty God cleanse us of our sins,
and through the eucharist we celebrate
make us worthy to sit at his table
in his heavenly kingdom.

The people answer:

Amen.

PENITENTIAL RITE(4)

After the introduction to the day's Mass, the priest invites the people to recall their sins and to repent of them in silence. He may use these or similar words:

Coming together as God's family,
with confidence let us ask the Father's
   forgiveness,
for he is full of gentleness and compassion.

A pause for silent reflection follows.

After the silence...all say:

I confess to almighty God,
and to you, my brother and sisters,
that I have sinned through my own fault

They strike their breast

in my thoughts and in my words,
in what I have done,
and in what I have failed to do;
and I ask blessed Mary, ever virgin,
all the angels and saints,
and you, my brothers and sisters,
to pray for me to the Lord our God.

The priest says the absolution:

May almighty God have mercy on us,
forgive us our sins,
and bring us to everlasting life.

The people answer:

Amen.

KYRIE(5)

V. Lord, have mercy.
R. Lord, have mercy.
V. Christ, have mercy.
R. Christ, have mercy.
V. Lord, have mercy.
R. Lord, have mercy.

(4) Silence at the beginning of the Blessing and Penitential Rite allows the people to recollect themselves and to offer time for an examination of conscience. There are three forms; Form A, the medieval Confiteor ("I confess...") is a clear expression of the communal dimension of repentance. Each of the forms starts with "the experience of our radical dependence on Christ" (Manly and Reinhard 248), either in the form of a plea for mercy or as a thanksgiving for that mercy. All three forms are wishes and requests, petitions for pardon. None are formulas for absolution and none is a substitute for the sacrament of reconciliation. The emphasis in all three is on God's mercy, mediated by Jesus Christ through his life, death and resurrection.

(5) The "Kyrie, eleison" is a song in litany form that acclaims and praises the Lord and implores him to be merciful. As often as possible, it should be sung, but if not sung, it should be recited. It is not to be eliminated, as it is an integral part of the Penitential Rite.

Intent: Penitential Rite through Opening Prayer (page 3)

GLORIA(6)

Glory to God in the highest,
  and peace to his people on earth.

Lord God, heavenly King,
almighty God and Father,
  we worship you, we give you thanks,
  we praise you for your glory.

Lord Jesus Christ, only Son of the Father,
Lord God, Lamb of God,
you take away the sin of the world:
  have mercy on us;
you are seated at the right hand of the Father:
  receive our prayer.

For you alone are the Holy One,
you alone are the Lord,
you alone are the Most High,
  Jesus Christ,
  with the Holy Spirit,
  in the glory of God the Father. Amen.

OPENING PRAYER(7)

*Afterwards, the priest, with hands joined,
sings or says:*

Let us pray
  [in Advent time
  with longing and waiting
  for the coming of the Lord].

Priest and people pray silently for a while.

*Then the priest extends his hands and sings
or says the opening prayer:*

Father in heaven,
our hearts desire the warmth of your love
and our minds are searching for the light of
  your Word.

Increase our longing for Christ our Savior
and give us the strength to grow in love,
that the dawn of his coming
may find us rejoicing in his presence
and welcoming the light of his truth.
We ask this in the name of Jesus the Lord.

The people respond:

Amen.

(6) The Gloria is "an ancient hymn in which the Church, assembled in the Holy Spirit, praises and entreats the Father and the Lamb" (GI 31). In its present form, it dates back to Pope Gregory the Great (sixth century). "In the Gloria, we are indeed praying in accordance with very ancient liturgical tradition" (Emminghaus 125). At the present time, it is not prayed during Advent and Lent. It is festive in nature and really needs to be sung so that the festivity of the piece reaches its fullest expression.

(7) The Opening Prayer concludes the Introductory Rites. It is often called a "Collect," which expresses very briefly the focus of the day. Silence precedes the prayer; this silence is intended to help us realize that we are in the presence of God. The prayer has a set structure: an invitation to pray, a period of silence, the prayer itself, and the "Amen." Although only the priest prays the prayer aloud, through the invitation ("Let us pray") we are united in that prayer together. The trinitarian nature of the prayer is expressed as a prayer to the Father, through the Son, prayed in the Spirit.

Session 3:
First Reading *through* Profession of Faith

God's word nourishes us, the worshiping assembly, and we proclaim our belief.

Schedule

Time	Description
5 minutes	Gathering Prayer
20 minutes	Teaching 1: History and Structure of the Liturgy of the Word
10 minutes	Teaching 2: Liturgical Exegesis of the Readings and the Psalm
10 minutes	Prayer 1: Preparation for the Word
40 minutes	Prayer 2: Proclamation of the Word
10 minutes	Break
15 minutes	Reflection: Profession of Faith
10 minutes	Group Process
5 minutes	Intent: Profession of Faith
25 minutes	Prayer 3: Prayer of Belief

Resource Sheets

Recommended Reading

◊ Marcheschi, "Don't Be a Pew Potato," *Praying* 38 (September/October 1990): 5-6.

◊ Steere, "Intercession: Caring for Souls," *Weavings* 4 (March-April 1989): 17-26.

Overview

This session covers the Liturgy of the Word from the First Reading through the Profession of Faith. This session is a time for helping people experience the fullness of Christ that is at the center of the Liturgy of the Word. This session is also a time for helping people name their beliefs and the importance of these beliefs to their own faith. Through this opportunity, people may see more clearly the connection between the Scriptures that they hear each week and their proclamation of personal/communal belief.

This session departs from the normal pattern of reflection and intent sheets for each part of the liturgy. Replacing the standard reflection sheet for the readings, psalm and homily is a prayer entitled "Proclamation of the Word." The intent sheet for the readings, psalm and homily is incorporated in Teaching 1, which includes instruction on the origins, background and structure of the readings and the psalm.

Teaching 2, which immediately follows Teaching 1, is an exegesis of the readings and psalm you select for the "Proclamation of the Word." This exegesis is meant to open up the readings for the listener so that he/she can participate more fully in the proclamation. Keep this in mind as you prepare for the teaching.

There are two other prayers in this session. The first is the Prayer of Preparation for the Word, which immediately precedes the "Proclamation of the Word." The other is an interactive prayer of belief.

The reflection for this session is medium length—seven questions—and looks at only the Profession of Faith. Don't let the length fool you; the questions have a great deal of depth and will require time to answer in a way that is thoughtful, reflective and meaningful.

Gathering Prayer

See Session 2, page 54, for Gathering Prayer.

Teaching 1: History and Structure of the Liturgy of the Word

The three main points to cover in this section are:

◊ Origins of the Liturgy of the Word

◊ How the readings and the psalm are selected and fit together

---

Presenter's Reflection Questions

As you prepare for Session 3, you might ponder or bring to prayer the following questions:

◊ What is your own experience of the proclamation of the Word? How does hearing the Scriptures proclaimed differ from reading them?

◊ How does your own hearing of the Scriptures affect what you believe?

◊ What has most affected all that you believe about church, God, the Catholic religion?

◊ Which people in your life have been instrumental in the formation of your beliefs?

◊ What strengthens your beliefs? What challenges them? How do you feel when you experience your beliefs being strengthened? Challenged?

◊ Importance of the Homily, the Profession of Faith, and the General Intercessions

Although you will not cover the General Intercessions until Session 4 (due to time constraints), mention them in this teaching as an integral response of the community to the readings. For this teaching, refer to the Resource Sheet entitled "Intent 1: First Reading *through* Homily," pages 88-90, keeping in mind that this teaching is broader than the material on the sheet. For additional material, consider the following:

For general background:

◊ Baldovin, "Bible and Liturgy: Their Interrelation," *Worship: City, Church and Renewal*, 216-224.

◊ *Lectionary for Mass: Introduction*, 1-10.

For origins:

◊ Emminghaus, *Eucharist: Essence, Form and Celebration*, 31-36.

For structure:

◊ *General Instruction of the Roman Missal*, 33-42.

◊ Johnson, *Word and Eucharist Handbook*, 38-50.

◊ *Lectionary for Mass: Introduction*, 11-23.

Teaching 2: Liturgical Exegesis of the Readings and the Psalm

We recommend the following three sources for your exegesis:

◊ Baldovin, "Bible and Liturgy: Their Interrelation," *Worship: City, Church and Renewal*, 216-224. Read this if you haven't already done so for your preparation for Teaching 1. Look in particular at the subsection entitled, "What Are We Reading?"

◊ Nocent, *The Liturgical Year*. There are four books in this series, organized by the liturgical year. You will need the book that contains the readings you have selected.

◊ Your favorite biblical commentary. We use *The New Jerome Biblical Commentary*. Look up the passages that you have selected to read. Although the proclamation of the Word is different from private reading or praying, a commentary provides a great deal of background that many people find interesting.

So shall my word be
   that goes forth from
   my mouth;
It shall not return to me
   void,
   but shall do my will,
   achieving the end for
   which I sent it.
                — Isaiah 55:11

The readings must
therefore be listened to
by all with reverence;
they make up a principal
element of the liturgy.
                — GI 9

Prayer 1: Preparation for the Word

Introduction

This prayer of preparation is a guided meditation that takes places in your prayer space or the church proper. It should take about ten minutes. What do we mean by "guided meditation?" For our purposes here, a guided meditation is one in which the presenter, by talking, guides the participants through a particular scene, action or memory. This particular prayer focuses on eyes, ears, mind and heart because they are the avenues through which we respond to the proclamation of the Word.

Outline

Your prayer of preparation might follow this procedure:

1. Process to prayer/church space.

2. Everyone sits in chairs/pews.

3. Introduce the prayer, making the following points:

   a. Explain that the intent of the prayer is to help us learn how to listen more completely to the proclamation of Scripture. To do this, we must use our ears, eyes, mind and heart.

   b. Invite people to close their eyes if they feel comfortable doing so.

   c. Ask them to follow along in their imaginations with what you suggest in the meditation, allowing memories and/or images to arise as they will, again as participants are comfortable doing so.

   d. Encourage participants to be free enough to not follow along with your suggestions if they feel that God is calling them to stop at a particular point or if something else seems more important at that particular moment.

   e. Be free enough yourself to let the Spirit guide each person in the way he/she needs to be guided.

   f. Let the participants know that you will be speaking throughout the meditation. If they find your voice distracting, tell them to try to ignore it (this is in keeping with the point immediately preceding this one).

4. Pray through the meditation, which is located in the Details below.

5. Conclude with song. We recommend listening to John Michael Talbot's "St. Theresa's Prayer" from *The Heart of the Shepherd*.

> When they hear the word of God and reflect deeply on it, the faithful receive the power to respond to it actively with full faith, hope, and charity through prayer and self-giving, and not only during Mass but in their entire Christian life.
> — LI 48

When the Scriptures are read in the Church, God himself is speaking to (God's) people, and Christ, present in his own word, is proclaiming the Gospel.

—GI 9

Presenter Preparation

Your own preparation for prayer should include the following:

◊ Bring a tape and tape deck/"boom box" if you have chosen to close the prayer with song.

◊ Bring a copy of your own guided meditation if you have chosen not to use the one provided here.

◊ Because Prayer 2 immediately follows, have everything you need for that prayer on hand.

Details

You may use the guided meditation below verbatim, create your own, or use another that is comfortable for you. As with the Gathering Prayer, pray through it slowly, keeping your voice nicely modulated and even. Pause for one or two seconds where you see the "...". A paragraph break indicates a slightly longer pause. These pauses allow the participants to do or envision what you are suggesting. Prayed slowly, this should take about six minutes. Practice and time yourself.

Begin by making yourself as comfortable as possible in your chair.

We will first focus our attention on hearing the Word of God proclaimed among us....Become more aware of your ears.... Gently draw your attention to your ears for a moment...how they feel attached to your head....With your ears you hear all kinds of sounds...words...music...laughter...crying...screaming...noise that is harsh...noise that is irritating...sound that is soothing...sound that is comforting....Give thanks to God for the gift of hearing.

Now focus on seeing the Word of God proclaimed among us....Become more aware of your eyes....Gently draw your attention to your eyes...how they feel in your head....With your eyes you see all kinds of things...vibrant colors and soft hues... rough textures and smooth surfaces...friends...and enemies... light shining in thickly wooded forests...birds in flight...and children playing....Give thanks to God for the gift of sight.

For "who has known the mind of the Lord, so as to counsel him?" But we have the mind of Christ.

— 1 Corinthians 2:16

Now focus on understanding the Word of God proclaimed among us....Become more aware of your mind....Gently draw your attention to your mind....With your mind you produce all kinds of mental activity...thoughts that explain things...questions about things you can't explain...kind thoughts...and jealous yearnings...exciting ideas...and imaginative plans... musings that help you understand who you are...and who God is....Give thanks to God for the gift of your mind.

Now focus on feeling the Word of God proclaimed among us....Become more aware of your heart....Gently draw your attention into your heart....Your heart contains all manner of feelings...feelings of love toward those whom you have grown deeply attached to...feelings of sadness when someone near you dies...or goes away...feelings of joy on special occasions such as a birthday or a holiday...feelings of fear when you are no longer in control of a given situation...feelings of exuberance when you do something you never thought you could....Give thanks to God for the gift of your heart.

Now give thanks to God for all of these parts of you...for your ears...for your eyes...for your mind...for your heart....Ask God to open your ears and your eyes...your mind and your heart... that you might hear...see...believe...and feel God's Word more fully and more completely....Let this become a prayer for you each and every day.

Conclude the meditation gently, inviting everyone to open his/her eyes. If you have chosen to close with a song, now is the time to play it.

Prayer 2: Proclamation of the Word

Introduction

This prayer is actually a full Proclamation of the Word and a singing/intonation of the psalm. We recommend that you follow the structure in the Sacramentary, using the appropriate acclamation and responses, sitting for the First and Second Readings and Psalm, and standing for the Alleluia and Gospel. Do not rush; the forty minutes allotted for this prayer can be broken into four ten-minute segments as follows:

1. First Reading, Psalm, Second Reading

2. Procession, Alleluia, Incensation, Gospel Reading

3. Silent Reflection

4. Dialogue Homily or Group Discussion

Before you begin, let the participants know that there will be a short silence after each reading and a ten-minute period for silent prayer after the Gospel is proclaimed.

Invite the participants to notice some of the things that you have discussed in this session so far. Allow sufficient silence after the First and Second Readings.

To conclude the experience, we suggest one of two things: a dialogue homily or a group discussion. A dialogue homily is one in

Ezra opened the scroll so that all people might see it...and, as he opened it, all the people rose. Ezra blessed the LORD, the great God, and all the people, their hands raised high, answered, "Amen, amen!"
— Nehemiah 8:5-6

The Church has honored the word of God and the eucharistic mystery with the same reverence, although not with the same worship, and has always and everywhere intended and endorsed such honor.
— LI 10

which each person may offer a brief reflection on the readings as he/she is so moved. Questions for group discussion may include:

◊ What was the overall experience like for you?

◊ What were you most aware of?

◊ Was the prayer of preparation helpful for you? If so, in what way?

◊ What happened to you during the silent prayer following the Gospel reading?

Outline

1. Proclaim the First Reading from the ambo/lectern. Follow with silence.

2. Sing or intone the psalm.

3. Proclaim the Second Reading from the ambo/lectern. Follow with silence.

4. Stand and sing the Alleluia (unless you are in the season of Lent; see GI, 37-39).

5. For the Gospel reading, we recommend that you process from the altar to the ambo with two participants bearing the censer and candles and another bearing the Book of Gospels (if your community does not have a special book for the Gospel, can you borrow one?). This is described in *General Instruction of the Roman Missal*, 89-95, and in *Lectionary for Mass: Introduction*, 17.

6. Follow the Gospel with a ten-minute period of silence for reflection. Play quiet instrumental music, if desired.

7. Conclude with a dialogue homily or return to your regular session space if you have chosen to close the experience with discussion.

Presenter Preparation

Your own preparation for prayer should include the following:

◊ Mark Lectionary at chosen readings.

◊ Make photocopies of the psalm intonation/setting you have chosen for all participants. (Remember to get permission to reprint, if necessary.)

◊ Place Book of Gospels on altar.

◊ Prepare censer or thurible.

◊ Have instrumental music ready if you have chosen this for the ten-minute period following the Gospel.

Be doers of the word and not hearers only, deluding yourselves.
— James 1:22

Details

There are no additional details for this prayer. Follow the format as it appears in the Sacramentary, which is reproduced in the Resource Sheet entitled "Intent 1: Readings, Psalm and Homily," pages 88-90.

Break

Reflection: Profession of Faith

Introduction

After the break, introduce the Profession of Faith. Begin by asking everyone to silently reflect on what the word "belief" means to them. After several moments of silence, read John 20:24-31, the passage on doubting Thomas:

> Thomas, called Didymus, one of the Twelve, was not with them when Jesus came. So the other disciples said to him, "We have seen the Lord." But he said to them, "Unless I see the mark of the nails in his hands and put my finger in the nailmarks and put my hand into his side, I will not believe."
>
> Now a week later his disciples were again inside and Thomas was with them. Jesus came, although the doors were locked, and stood in their midst and said, "Peace be with you." Then he said to Thomas, "Put your finger here and see my hands, and bring your hand and put it into my side, and do not be unbelieving, but believe." Thomas answered and said to him, "My Lord and my God!" Jesus said to him, "Have you come to believe because you have seen me? Blessed are those who have not seen and have believed."
>
> Now Jesus did many other signs in the presence of [his] disciples that are not written in this book. But these are written that you may [come to] believe that Jesus is the Messiah, the Son of God, and that through this belief you may have life in his name.

Following this reading, distribute the reflection sheet, photocopied from page 91, to each participant.

Group Process

We recommend regular group sharing around the reflection questions.

As an expression of belief, the creed is professed by the whole assembly in response to the word just proclaimed in the readings and preached in the homily....It is a moment to give a resounding "yes" to the unending and marvelous works of God on our behalf.
— Johnson 55

Blessed are those who have not seen and have believed.
— John 20:29

Intent: Profession of Faith

Lead your discussion based on the intent sheet, page 92.

Prayer 3: Prayer of Belief

Introduction

This prayer draws out and reflects upon the gift of belief. This prayer will work within your regular session space.

Outline

1. Invite each person to meditate for several moments on what personal belief seems to feel like the most important for him/her at this particular moment

2. Pass paper and pencils around the circle, asking each person to take one of each.

3. Ask each person to write his/her personal belief on the paper.

4. Pass the basket around the circle, at which time each person may or may not choose to read his/her belief before placing it in the basket.

5. After each person places his/her belief in the basket, he/she holds the basket up slightly and everyone responds, "Blessed are they who have not seen and have believed."

6. Once the basket comes full circle, presenter raises the basket slightly and offers a prayer of thanksgiving for the gift of belief.

7. Conclude with Prayer of Belief.

Presenter Preparation

Your own preparation for prayer should include the following:

◊ Provide small pieces of paper and a pencil for each participant.

◊ Bring a small basket.

◊ Bring a closing prayer of thanksgiving. (See #6 in Outline above.)

◊ Photocopy the Prayer of Belief, pages 93-94, for each person.

"Lord, save me!" Immediately Jesus stretched out his hand and caught him, and said to him, "O you of little faith, why did you doubt?"

— Matthew 14:30-31

Details

Before you begin the prayer, it might be a good idea to explain the process first, as it is written in the outline above. Ask for two volunteers to be Reader 1 and Reader 2 for the Prayer of Belief. Allow about ten minutes for meditation and for each person to write down his/her belief. It may take some time for people to put their belief into words. Make sure everyone feels free not to read their belief. Once each person places his/her belief in the basket, the entire community prays in unison, "Blest are they...." These words should be prayed slowly and reverently. Then the person passes the basket on.

Once the basket has come full circle, conclude this portion of the experience with a prayer, again elevating the basket slightly in a gesture of honor and reverence. Feel the offering and reverence with your body. The group will notice this. The prayer may be as simple as, "Thank you, God, this day/night for the gift of belief you have bestowed upon us." It may be longer if you choose; you might want to use the following:

> Loving God, our beliefs are your gift to us. We praise you. We give you thanks for all the beliefs we have placed in this basket this day. We ask you to continue to strengthen our belief in you, in Jesus and in the Holy Spirit. May our belief in you grow as strong as the stately oaks that lift their limbs to you, as firm as the earth that supports our footsteps, as never-ending as the waves that wash upon the beach. We pray this in Jesus' name. Amen.

Conclude the experience with the Prayer of Belief.

This prayer concludes Session 3.

Falling down before (Jesus), she explained in the presence of all the people why she had touched him and how she had been healed immediately. He said to her, "Daughter, your faith has saved you; go in peace."

— Luke 8:47-48

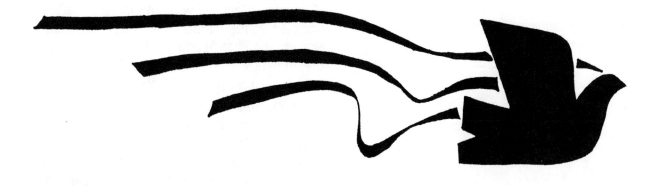

Session 3 Resource Sheets

Intent 1: First Reading *through* Homily

LITURGY OF THE WORD(1)

FIRST READING(2)

The reader goes to the lectern for the first reading. All sit and listen. To indicate the end, the reader adds:

The Word of the Lord.

All respond:

Thanks be to God.

RESPONSORIAL PSALM(3)

The cantor sings or recites the psalm, and the people respond.

SECOND READING(4)

When there is a second reading, it is read at the lectern as before. To indicate the end, the reader adds:

The Word of the Lord.

All respond:

Thanks be to God.

(1) The Liturgy of the Word consists of the First and Second Readings, the Responsorial Psalm, the Alleluia acclamation, the Gospel, the Homily, the Profession of Faith and the General Interecessions. "In the readings, explained by the homily, God is speaking to his people, opening up to them the mystery of redemption and salvation, and nourishing their spirit" (GI 33). The Gospel readings follow a three-year cycle: Matthew is read in Cycle A; Mark and John in Cycle B; Luke in Cycle C.

(2) In response to the mandate in *The Constitution on the Sacred Liturgy* that "the treasures of the Bible are to be opened up more lavishly, so that a richer share of God's word may be provided for the faithful" (51), Vatican II's reforms called for three readings (GI 318). The revised Lectionary appeared in 1969. The First Reading is usually in accord with the Gospel reading, complementing its message. During the Easter Season, the First Reading is taken from Acts of the Apostles; during the rest of the liturgical year, it is taken from the Hebrew Scriptures.

(3) The psalm is both the people's response to and meditation on the First Reading. This follows Jewish synagogue practice, in which "the community traditionally replies to a scriptural reading by singing a psalm or biblical canticle" (Johnson 40). Prior to Vatican II, the Responsorial Psalm was known as the Gradual. It should be sung where possible. The common methods of singing are: (1) the cantor sings the verses and the people sing the response; (2) the cantor or choir sings the complete psalm and the people listen; (3) the entire assembly sings the complete psalm.

(4) The Second Reading usually has no connection to either the First Reading or the Gospel. It stands alone as a reading usually taken from the apostolic letters. The selections are often sequential; for example, in Cycle A we hear excerpts from Romans for sixteen consecutive weeks.

Intent 1: First Reading through Homily (page 2)

ALLELUIA OR GOSPEL ACCLAMATION(5)

The alleluia or other chant follows. It is to be omitted if not sung.

Cantor/Assembly: Alleluia. Alleluia.

Cantor: Lord, let us see your kindness, and grant us your salvation.

Assembly: Alleluia. Alleluia.

GOSPEL(6)

Meanwhile, if incense is used, the priest puts some in the censer. Then the deacon who is to proclaim the gospel bows to the priest and in a low voice asks his blessing:

Father, give me your blessing.

The priest says in a low voice:

The Lord be in your heart and on your lips that you may worthily proclaim his gospel. In the name of the Father and of the Son, ✠ and of the Holy Spirit.

The deacon answers:

Amen.

If there is no deacon, priest bows before the altar and says inaudibly:

Almighty God, cleanse my heart and my lips that I may worthily proclaim your gospel.

Then the deacon (or the priest) goes to the lectern. He may be accompanied by ministers with incense and candles. He sings or says:

The Lord be with you.

The people answer:

And also with you.

The deacon (or priest) sings or says:

A reading from the holy gospel according to N.

He makes the sign of the cross on the book, and then on his forehead, lips and breast.(7)
The people respond:

Glory to you, Lord.

Then, if incense is used, the deacon (or priest) incenses the book, and proclaims the gospel.

(5) This exclamation of the people is not a perfunctory response but an expression of joy that looks forward to the Gospel. "Alleluia" is a word taken from the Hebrew and literally means "Praise ye, Yahweh." The verse betweeen the sung alleluias should reflect the message of the Gospel. The Alleluia is sung in every season except for Lent, when a simple verse such as, "Glory and praise to you, Lord Jesus Christ!" is used in its place.

(6) The Gospel is the high point of the Liturgy of the Word. That is why we stand, why we use incense at this point, why many communities have a special book called *The Book of Gospels.* "The Gospel stands for Christ himself, who through his word is present in his community" (Emminghaus 144).

(7) The signing of the cross is done as well by the people and may be accompanied by words prayed silently in the hearts of every believer: "May the words of the Lord be in my mind, on my lips and in my heart."

Intent 1: First Reading through Homily (page 3)

At the end of the gospel, the deacon (or priest) adds:

The gospel of the Lord.

All respond:

Praise to you, Lord Jesus Christ.

Then he kisses the book, saying inaudibly,

May the words of the gospel wipe away our sins.

HOMILY(8)

A homily shall be given on all Sundays and holy days of obligation; it is recommended for other days.

(8) The Homily (from the Latin *homilia*, "conversation") has roots in the Jewish synagogue service. It should not be omitted and, as a rule, its purpose is to break open the Scriptures so that they become the living Word for a particular assembly in a given time and place. The needs of the people need to be taken into consideration during homily preparation, and "the homily [needs to] be truly the fruit of meditation" (LI 24). Although many assemblies have grown used to having the homily frequently given by someone other than the presider, the *Lectionary for Mass: Introduction* states, "As a rule it is to be given by the one presiding" (24).

In masses with children, the documents have made provision for an adult other than the priest to speak to the children when it has been deemed appropriate (DMC 24).

Reflection: Profession of Faith

PROFESSION OF FAITH

We believe(1) in one God,
   the Father,(2) the Almighty,
   maker of heaven and earth,
   of all that is seen and unseen.

We believe in one Lord, Jesus Christ,(3)
   the only Son of God,
   eternally begotten of the Father,
   God from God, Light from Light,
   true God from true God,
   begotten, not made, one in Being with the
      Father.
   Through him, all things were made.
   For us men and for our salvation
      he came down from heaven:

All bow during these two lines:

by the power of the Holy Spirit
   he was born of the Virgin Mary, and
      became man.

For our sake he was crucified under Pontius
      Pilate;
   he suffered, died and was buried.
   On the third day he rose again
      in fulfillment of the Scriptures;
   he ascended into heaven
      and is seated at the right hand of the
         Father.
He will come again in glory to judge the
      living and the dead,
   and his kingdom will have no end.(4)

We believe in the Holy Spirit,(5) the Lord, the
      giver of life,
   who proceeds from the Father and the Son.
   With the Father and the Son he is
      worshipped and glorified.
   He has spoken through the Prophets.
   We believe in one holy catholic and
      apostolic(6) Church.
   We acknowledge one baptism for the
      forgiveness of sins.
We look for the resurrection of the dead,
   and the life of the world to come(7). Amen.

(1) What does it mean for you to believe? How does it make you feel?

(2) How do you experience the presence of the Father?

(3) How do you experience the presence of the Son, Jesus Christ?

(4) Of all of the beliefs about Jesus in this part of our Profession of Faith, which one is the most meaningful for you and why?

(5) How do you experience the presence of the Holy Spirit?

(6) What do these four things—"one, holy, catholic, apostolic"—mean to you? Which evokes the strongest feeling for you?

(7) How does proclaiming all the beliefs professed in the creed aid you on your journey?

Intent 2: Profession of Faith

PROFESSION OF FAITH

We believe in one God,
   the Father, the Almighty
   maker of heaven and earth,
   of all that is seen and unseen.

We believe in one Lord, Jesus Christ,
   the only Son of God,
   eternally begotten of the Father,
   God from God, Light from Light,
   true God from true God,
   begotten, not made, one in Being with the
      Father.
   Through him all things were made.
   For us men and for our salvation
      he came down from heaven:

All bow during these two lines:

by the power of the Holy Spirit
   he was born of the Virgin Mary, and
      became man.

For our sake he was crucified under Pontius
      Pilate;
   he suffered, died and was buried.
   On the third day he rose again
      in fulfillment of the Scriptures;
   he ascended into heaven
      and is seated at the right hand of the
         Father.
He will come again in glory to judge the
      living and the dead,
   and his kingdom will have no end.

We believe in the Holy Spirit, the Lord, the
      giver of life,
   who proceeds from the Father and the Son.
   With the Father and the Son he is
      worshipped and glorified.
   He has spoken through the Prophets.
   We believe in one holy catholic and
      apostolic Church.
   We acknowledge one baptism for the
      forgiveness of sins.
   We look for the resurrection of the dead,
      and the life of the world to come. Amen.

At first glance, the Profession of Faith can be seen as a recitation of beliefs, but it is far more than that. It is our assent, our "yes" and our "amen" to what we have heard in the readings and in the homily (see GI 43). It is also a recognition of our belief in not only the gathered people but also in all Christians for all of time.

By reciting a prayer, a creed, that was written more than fifteen centuries ago, we unite ourselves with those Christians and with their beliefs as well.

"Our hearty recital of these phrases, and the whole Creed, is an opportunity to express our grateful solidarity with...all Christians and ultimately to Jesus Christ" (Manly and Reinhard 259).

Gregory Manly and Anneliese Reinhard call the Profession of Faith our faith-anthem. If we allow ourselves to be carried by this anthem, our feelings will be similar to those we have when we sing our national anthem. We will have a feeling of bonding, a feeling of thanksgiving, a feeling of pride that we belong to the Church. A wealth of experience is packed into this prayer.

Our Profession of Faith, commonly called the Nicene Creed, is handed down to us from the Council of Nicea (325 A.D.). It also has roots in the Council of Constantinople, which occurred later on in that century.

The Creed was formulated as a reaction to the teaching of Arius, who was a fourth-century Egyptian priest. He taught that Jesus was a superior being but not equal to the Father. To counteract this belief, the Council declared that Christ was one in being with the Father but not identical with Him. The Creed was accepted by the papacy formally in the eleventh century.

Originally, the Creed was used during the Rite of Baptism but not during celebrations of the Eucharist. Once it began to be used in the Mass, it became obligatory to sing or recite it on Sundays and solemnities. It may be used during other solemn occasions as well.

Prayer of Belief [1]

All: **Blest are they who have not seen and have believed.**

Reader 1: Listen!
Let the saddened and despaired lift their eyes;
Let those whose hearts are heavy breathe freely.
Let them birth forth new children in hope;
    and care for their young in promise.

All: **Blest are they who have not seen and have believed.**

Reader 2: A new age is opening before us,
    an age of oneness and peace,
Where we shall see in each other
    a new vision fresh as a first moment.

All: **Blest are they who have not seen and have believed.**

Reader 1: Tell all you know to take courage
    to claim inner power and strength.
There is no need to be overwhelmed or to fear;
    darkness is but prelude to dawn.

All: **Blest are they who have not seen and have believed.**

Reader 2: The drugged and addicted will awaken
    with integrity where idols fall.
Limbs paralyzed with indecision and fear
    will now walk unencumbered and free.

All: **Blest are they who have not seen and have believed.**

Reader 1: Rejoice!
The poor will be poor no longer;
    the rich will be rich in deed.
And for those who wander our street, weary:
    the misfortuned will be nourished,
    the elderly and the lost, received.

All: **Blest are they who have not seen and have believed.**

Reader 2: No longer
    will neighborhoods be wary and armed
    nor leaders vigilant with mistrust.
No longer
    will resources be burdened with war
    and our youth conditioned to violence.

All: **Blest are they who have not seen and have believed.**

---

[1] Reprinted with permission from Bergan and Schwan, *Freedom*, 57-59.

Prayer of Belief (page 2)

Reader 1: A new age is upon us;
A new way unfolding
        —beyond détente, beyond force—
Forgiveness will crumble walls;
        trust become the builder of cities.

All: Blest are they who have not seen and have believed.

Reader 2: Reverence will be the blessing
        embracing our entire planet.
Never, never war in the stars!
        Magi satellites will network a communion and message of love.

All: Blest are they who have not seen and have believed.

Reader 1: Rejoice!
The earth will be renewed.
As ancient redwoods stand in surety,
        And quakes are gentled by prayer.
Then land, once shackled and dormant with mortgage,
        will sevenfold yield its abundance.
The earth will be renewed!

All: Blest are they who have not seen and have believed.

Reader 2: Pure water for the many: fresh, clean
        nourishing life deep within.
All deserts, wastelands watered,
        all thirsty fires quenched.
The earth will be renewed and live!

All: Blest are they who have not seen and have believed.

Reader 1: Dare to dream; creation is upon us.
        Death's door has been slammed shut.
The end, though forecast as doom,
        is—oh, joy—joy!

All: Blest are they who have not seen and have believed.

Reader 2: Listen! Jesus is come, risen, alive.
        He brings new hope, promises fulfilled.
The path he walks is a highway for us.
        Through chaos and ashes, his Spirit leads.

All: Blest are they who have not seen and have believed.

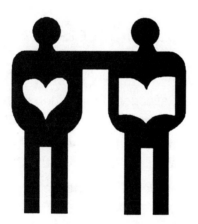

Session 4:
General Intercessions *through* Prayer over the Gifts

*As the worshiping assembly, we conclude the Liturgy of the Word by praying
with and for each other, and we begin the Liturgy of the Eucharist.*

Schedule

Time	Description
5 minutes	Gathering Prayer
5 minutes	Intent 1: General Intercessions
40 minutes	Prayer 1: Intercessory Prayer
15 minutes	Reflection: Preparation of the Altar and the Gifts *through* Prayer over the Gifts
10 minutes	Break
20 minutes	Group Process
15 minutes	Intent 2: Preparation of the Altar and the Gifts *through* Prayer over the Gifts
40 minutes	Prayer 2: Presentation of Gifts

Resource Sheets

Recommended Reading

◊ Manly and Reinhard, "Sacrifice," *Art of Praying Liturgy*, 279-283.

◊ Pleiness, "You and I Are Eucharist," *Living Prayer* 21 (May-June 1988): 18-21.

Overview

This session concludes the Liturgy of the Word with an exploration of the General Intercessions. The examples provided are general intercessions that would be used during the Season of Advent. Point out some of the images of the season that appear in this prayer—darkness and light, peace and preparation—which set the prayer firmly within the context of the season.

There is no reflection sheet for the General Intercessions. Rather than reflect on the intercessions themselves, you will use an intercessory form of prayer that is personal and also communal.

Begin the session with a brief explanation of the history, structure and intent of the General Intercessions, and then move right into the Intercessory Prayer, which will take approximately forty minutes, depending upon the size of the group.

After the prayer, there are reflection sheets (eight questions) for the Preparation of the Altar and Gifts *through* Prayer over the Gifts, a break, and then group process around these reflections. Follow this with an explanation of the Preparation of the Altar and the Gifts. The session will conclude with a second prayer experience, again lasting about forty minutes, around the Presentation of the Gifts.

The session is fairly straightforward—no teaching other than that involved in the intent on the General Intercessions and the Preparation of the Altar and the Gifts and the Presentation of the Gifts, about twenty minutes in all.

For supplementary reading on the General Intercessions and the Preparation of the Gifts, consider the following:

◊ Emminghaus, *Eucharist: Essence, Form, Celebration,* 151-154; 157-168.

◊ Johnson, *Word & Eucharist Handbook,* 57-61; 67-78.

◊ *General Instruction of the Roman Missal,* 45-47; 49-53; 101-107; 235.d.

◊ *Appendix to the General Instruction,* 50.

◊ *Music in Catholic Worship,* 46.

◊ Zimmerman, "The General Intercessions: Yet Another Visit," *Worship* 65 (May 1993): 239-252.

◊ Krosnicki, "Preparing the Gifts: Clarifying the Rite," *Worship* 65 (March 1991): 149-159.

Presenter's Reflection Questions

As you prepare for Session 4, you might ponder or bring to prayer the following questions:

◊ What is it like for you to pray for others? What is it like for you to ask others to pray for you?

◊ What do you perceive as God's gifts to you? To your faith community?

◊ How do you celebrate those gifts?

◊ How do you encourage others to recognize and celebrate their own?

When (we) enter the prayer of intercession (we) do it with an acute realization that (we are) only adding (our) caring to the cosmic love of a God who cares.

— Steere 17

Gathering Prayer

See Session 2, page 54, for Gathering Prayer.

Intent 1: General Intercessions

Lead your discussion based on the intent sheet beginning on page 106.

Prayer 1: Intercessory Prayer

What was the most significant prayer experience for you?

The intercessory prayer was one of the experiences I enjoyed— the idea of my petition being prayed to help me as an individual was new; the partner sharing was also helpful in articulating particular needs not always verbalized.

— A Participant

Introduction

This form of intercessory prayer is both intimately personal and communal at the same time. First, invite each participant to go within him/herself and identify a need for which to pray. Then ask him/her to communicate that need to a prayer partner, who will pray for that need. Finally, ask each person to present his/her partner's need to the entire group so that you can pray for this need communally.

This can be a powerful experience of intercessory prayer if done well and with enough explanation so that people are comfortable with the process. Allow at least five minutes to do a "dry run" with the group so that they know what they are supposed to do. Prayer is difficult if everyone is confused. (God can only help to a certain point!) You may use the scenario in the Details section to demonstrate the process.

The Intercessory Prayer was a turning point for those in our program, which was both a surprise and a great gift. In a way that is hard to put into words, it solidified the bond that had been growing between all of us during the previous three weeks. It was a reverent, intimate experience for the group.

Outline

1. Explain the prayer to the group, making sure everyone is clear about the process.

2. Establish prayer "teams."

3. Each person prays alone for a specific amount of time, during which he/she opens his/her heart to a pressing need in either his/her own life or a need in the world with which he/she is concerned.

4. Prayer partners turn to or find each other and share their particular needs or stories.

5. Each partner prays for the other, silently or out loud.

6. The whole group gathers and each person asks for prayers on behalf of his/her partner.

Presenter Preparation

You need no special things—paper, prayer handouts, etc.—for this prayer.

Details

How you establish prayer teams is up to you. You may simply ask each person to turn to the person sitting next to him/her. You may also ask each person to find a prayer partner from anywhere within the group. Or you may come up with some creative method that we simply have not considered. (Let us know about it!)

Once each person has a prayer partner, invite everyone to pray quietly for between five and ten minutes. You will have a sense by now of how long people are comfortable praying alone. Give them the freedom to leave the room or walk around or find a suitable quiet space within which to pray. If it looks like people are going to wander, give them a designated time to return. Ask the participants to find a need in their life or in the world that might need prayer at this moment. Encourage them to invite God into the process and make their prayer personal and intimate.

After this five- to ten-minute period of quiet prayer, have the people come together and form prayer teams so that they may pray for each other. How does this work? Teams disperse into corners and nooks to find some privacy. One partner begins by sharing his/her need with his/her partner. This may take several minutes. Then the one who is listening offers prayer for that person. This prayer can be either silent or out loud. When the listener is done praying, the roles are reversed. Allow ten minutes for this portion of the prayer.

Gather everyone into a large group. Go around the group and have each person intercede for their partner. Use the familiar format of the General Intercessions:

◊ State the need.

◊ Follow with a moment of silence during which each person takes that need into his/her heart.

◊ The person stating the need prays, "For this we pray to the Lord."

◊ The group responds together with the words, "Lord, hear our prayer."

How does this whole process look in real life? Let's say that Sarah and Jim are partners. In Sarah's quiet time, the issue that comes to

> The general intercessions are one appreciable way the liturgy brings home its claim to make the good news present in everyday life for everyone and for all times.
> — Zimmerman 312

> In the general intercessions or prayer of the faithful, the people, *exercising their priestly function*, intercede for all humanity.
> — GI 45 (my emphasis).

By praying with others, we find a support which most of us need and cannot get from praying alone.

— Steindl-Rast 57

There is no form of prayer that is more obvious an act of real love than the costly act of intercessory prayer.

— Steere 25

her in prayer is that of her son. Sarah shares with Jim the story of her son's difficulties at school and how hard this has been for her. She asks Jim to pray for her, for her son, and for her son's teachers, that everyone involved may have a greater sense of understanding and patience.

Jim prays silently for Sarah and when he is finished, he begins to share his own story or need with her. He shares with Sarah his increasing awareness of a conflict in a third-world country. He has a friend who just returned from there, and his friend's stories make the horror more real and immanent for Jim. He cannot believe the injustice, and he is especially sad for the children there. He feels helpless. He asks Sarah to pray for these children and for the world, that all may find peace.

Sarah prays out loud for him, in her own words. They join the larger group.

In the context of the large group, there is no need to share each person's entire story. First, it would take too long. Second, it might feel invasive or like a breach of confidence, especially if the one-on-one sharing has been intimate. When it is Sarah's turn, she says simply, "Jim would like us to pray for the children in warring countries, that we may find ways to help them." She pauses for a moment, then continues, "For this we pray to the Lord." The group responds, "Lord, hear our prayer."

When it is Jim's turn, he says to the large group, "Let us pray for Sarah, that God might grant her greater patience and understanding. For this we pray to the Lord." The group responds, "Lord, hear our prayer." For this portion of the prayer, it is easiest and least confusing to go around the circle in sequential order.

Reflection: Preparation of the Altar and the Gifts *through* Prayer over the Gifts

Distribute the reflections sheets, photocopied from pages 108-109, to each participant.

Break

Group Process

We recommend a form of regular group sharing around the reflection questions.

Intent 2: Preparation of the Altar and the Gifts *through* Prayer over the Gifts

Lead your discussion based on the intent sheet beginning on page 110.

Prayer 2: Presentation of Gifts

Introduction

This prayer involves a personal experience of presenting the gifts at the table of the Lord. More specifically, each person will be asked to present his/herself to God. I once heard someone say that not only do we bring the gifts of bread and wine to the altar, but we place ourselves there as well. This gave me great pause, and I began to wonder what it would be like to actually experience that moment with our own bodies. This prayer stems from that desire.

We recommend that you begin with some general discussion of what it means to offer sacrifice and what gifts God has given to us. Then process in silence to your designated prayer space with altar, sit before the altar, pray and present yourselves. The prayer will take about forty minutes, depending upon the size of your group.

Outline

1. Introduce the prayer with a brief discussion of sacrifice and gift, following the suggestions found in the opening remarks of the Details below.

2. Process to prayer space.

3. Explain the prayer.

4. Begin with the Prayer of Acceptance.

5. Each person makes his/her presentation at the altar.

6. Individuals return to their seats if there are chairs in the prayer space; if not, individuals return to the places where they were standing until all people have presented themselves.

7. Close prayer with song. We recommend "Take, Lord, Receive" by John Foley.

Presenter Preparation

Your own preparation for prayer should include the following:

◊ Prepare an outline or "script" of what you plan to say to introduce the prayer.

> (B)y offering the immaculate Victim, not only through the hands of the priest, but also with him, (Christ's faithful) should learn to offer themselves as well.
> — CSL 48

◊ Have a photocopy of the Prayer of Acceptance on hand.

◊ If you choose to close the prayer with a song, make copies of the text of the song (remember to get reprint permission, if necessary).

Details

Begin the prayer with a brief explanation of what "sacrifice" means. We offer you the following text, which you may read or paraphrase or from which you may draw your own ideas:

Opening Remarks

Discussion of Sacrifice and Gift: This first part of the Liturgy of the Eucharist plunges us into the most complex symbols of the liturgy—those of sacrifice and gift. In order to help us understand and participate more fully in this preparation, the eucharistic prayers and communion, I would like to spend some time first talking about offering sacrifice and what we mean by "gift."

Throwing Out Our Old Definitions about Sacrifice: Most of us have a good idea of what we mean when we talk about sacrifice. I am sure that there are very few among us who, as children, did not hear our parents at one time or another talk about how much they had sacrificed for us. This, of course, was spoken to us to help us feel thankful for what they had done but often resulted in helping us feel guilty about one thing or another. Most of us who are parents swore that we would never say that sort of thing to our children. But how often do we find ourselves sneaking in that kind of comment? How easily it just slips out. This use of "sacrifice" is so prevalent that is it difficult to get away from it. Webster's dictionary defines sacrifice in terms of giving up; the synonyms it suggests are "loss" and "deprivation."

Sacrifice As an Acknowledgment of God's Many Gifts to Us: When we switch gears and move to the celebration of the Mass—we refer to it as the "Holy Sacrifice of the Mass"—these definitions of "loss" and "deprivation" do not fit. We need to discover a different meaning of sacrifice; we need to look at the Hebrew usage of "sacrifice" in the Jewish Scriptures. When Jewish people offered sacrifice to their God, what they were doing was acknowledging and accepting God's own gift to them. What the Jews were acknowledging was the gift of relationship—"you shall be my people, and I will be your God" (Ez 36:28)—the gift of the covenant. If the sacrifice was made to atone for sin, then the sacrifice was renewing, reestablishing the relationship with God. Sacrifice could also be offered to

---

...through Christ the Mediator, (Christ's faithful) should be formed day by day into an ever more perfect unity with God and with each other, so that finally God may be all in all.

— CSL 48

In the name of the people who love me, I offer to our Father the gifts of the lives of the lovers gathered.

— Pleiness 20

strengthen the relationship. We, too, need to look at sacrifice as a form of acknowledging and giving, not as a process of giving up something (all too often in a begrudging manner).

Sacrifice As Our "Yes" to God: The Holy Sacrifice of the Mass is our way of saying "yes" to God, our response to God. It is joy-filled celebration, praise and thanksgiving for all that God gives us, particularly a renewed covenant and life through Jesus, God's son. Liturgy, more specifically the Liturgy of the Eucharist, is our way of remembering and thanking God for this covenant, this relationship God gives us with and through Jesus. Jesus' own "yes" to God was the most profound expression of this meaning of sacrifice—his crucifixion, death and resurrection offered in total love and obedience.

Sacrifice in Imitation of Christ: How can we best offer sacrifice, best say "yes" to God's gift of a renewed covenant with us? We can choose to imitate Jesus—offer our own selves to God to serve God's people as Jesus did. We no longer live in an age, at least in America, where martyrdom is common, so this does not often involve physical suffering, death and resurrection. Our offering is symbolic. We figuratively die to self, to our own selfish desires and needs, so that we might unite ourselves to the living Christ within each of us: "I have been crucified with Christ; yet I live, no longer I, but Christ lives in me" (Gal 2:19-20). We must realize that Christ has no physical form now; we surrender ourselves to him and in so doing we become his Body.

Acknowledging God's Gifts to Us by Presenting Ourselves to God: And what of gift? It is God who gives to us, make no mistake. We can do nothing more but receive and offer thanks and praise for these gifts. Jesus is God's greatest gift to us, made present to us in the form of bread and wine. Our response to this gift is to offer sacrifice—*to say yes*—by turning to God and presenting to God the first fruits of this gift, fruit of the vine, ourselves. As we present the bread and the wine, we begin the process by which we unite ourselves to this gift from God. As we watch people from the assembly present the gifts during the Preparation of the Altar and the Gifts, we symbolically present ourselves as well.

Process to Prayer Space/Church

The group processes in silence to the prayer space/church, where you will begin to pray.

Lord, hear the prayers of your people and receive our gifts. May the worship of each one here bring salvation to all.
— Prayer over the Gifts, 24th Sunday in Ordinary Time

Given
In
Freedom and
Thanksgiving for our
Salvation

Lord,
look with love on our
    service.
Accept the gifts we bring
and help us grow in
    Christian love.
Grant this through Christ
    our Lord.
    — Prayer over the Gifts,
        Tenth Sunday
        in Ordinary Time

Merciful Lord,
make holy these gifts,
and let our spiritual
    sacrifice
make us an everlasting
    gift to you.
We ask this in the name
    of Jesus the Lord.
    — Prayer over the Gifts,
        Eighteenth Sunday
        in Ordinary Time

Prayer Sequence

When everyone is assembled in the space, give a few simple instructions, including the following:

◊ Ask them to quietly walk out of the pews/seats and approach the altar from the center aisle. Remind them to be mindful and prayerful as they approach the altar. Their action of presenting themselves to God as self-gift is prayer.

◊ Tell them that, as presider, you will stand at the front of the altar, ready to receive each person. You will offer a prayer for this gift of self as each arrives at the altar.

◊ Once each person has presented him/herself, he/she will return to the pew/chair for a few moments of silent meditation. Following the meditation, you may want to conclude with a song.

After you have completed this basic explanation, invite them into prayer. Use the Prayer of Acceptance on page 112 or a similar prayer.

Individual Presentation

After you pray together, invite the first person to come forward. As he/she arrives in front of the altar, place your hand on his/her shoulder as a gesture of reception and welcome and pray these or similar words:

Lord, God,
Receive your child, N.,
and be pleased with her/him
    as she/he presents her/himself to you.
Prepare her/him to become one with Jesus
    and one with the community.

Closing Song

When all have presented themselves and you have sung, return to your regular session space.

This concludes Session 4.

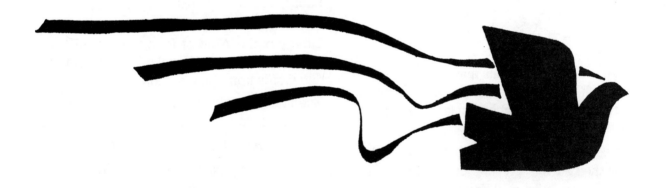

Session 4 Resource Sheets

Intent 1: General Intercessions

GENERAL INTERCESSIONS

The priest presides at the prayer. With a brief introduction, he invites the people to pray; after the intentions he says the concluding prayer.

It is desirable that the intentions be announced by the deacon, cantor, or other person.

Priest: Many people throughout the world live in darkness because of ignorance and weakness, persecution and deprivation. Enlightened by the Word of the Lord, we pray that the light of justice will disperse their darkness.

Deacon: Please respond to our prayers of petition with, "Come, Lord Jesus."

Deacon: That our church may become a beacon of peace and justice, a voice crying in the wilderness of the world, "Prepare ye the way," we pray to the Lord.

Deacon: That all nations may work toward the birth of a more lasting peace and an end to the violent ways of humankind, we pray to the Lord.

Deacon: For families throughout the world, may their Advent preparations lead them into a deeper experience of Emmanuel, "God-with-us," we pray to the Lord.

Deacon: That we may set aside quiet time to prepare for Jesus' coming through meditation and prayer this Advent season, we pray to the Lord.

Deacon: That all who answer death's call this week rest in Jesus, the Lord of light, we pray to the Lord.

Deacon: For the sick in our community and for those who care for them, that the hope and light and joy of this season will penetrate their darkness and bring them comfort, we pray to the Lord.

The General Intercessions are offered at every Mass. This is a prayer of the assembly, a prayer of the faithful, an opportunity for the people to exercise their "priestly function" by virtue of their baptism. God calls us to pray for all of humanity, not just for those present in the assembly (see GI 45).

Manly and Reinhard suggest that the feeling aimed for in intercessory prayer can best be experienced when the intercessions come spontaneously from the assembly. This is not possible when the assembly is large; it would cause the intercessions to be disproportionate to the rest of the Liturgy of the Word.

The intercessions serve to link the Liturgy of the Word to the Liturgy of the Eucharist because the intentions are repeated during the Liturgy of the Eucharist.

These intercessions should grow out of the Liturgy of the Word or from the special Mass, be it a marriage, a funeral, etc., using images and words from the readings of the day.

The litany form that we use follows the same order each day:

◊ an opening prayer by the priest

◊ the intercessions, following a usual sequence (GI 46):

  1. for the needs of the Church

  2. for public authorities and world salvation

  3. for those oppressed by any need

  4. for the local community

◊ following each intention, an invitation from the lector/deacon/priest to pray to the Lord.

◊ a short period of silence for that prayer

◊ a spoken communal response, e.g., "We pray to the Lord."

Intent 1: General Intercessions (page 2)

Deacon: For those intentions that we hold
deep within our hearts, we pray to the Lord.

Priest: Father, source of light and strength,
you instruct us in your ways
and guide us through life.
Look upon us and hear our requests.
We ask this through Christ our Lord.

Reflection: Preparation of the Altar and the Gifts *through* Prayer over the Gifts

LITURGY OF THE EUCHARIST

PREPARATION OF THE ALTAR AND THE GIFTS(1)

After the liturgy of the word, the offertory song is begun. Meanwhile the ministers place the corporal, the purificator, the chalice, and the missal on the altar.

It is desirable that the participation of the faithful be expressed by members of the congregation bringing up the bread and wine for the celebration of the eucharist or other gifts(2) for the needs of the Church and the poor.

The priest, standing at the altar, takes the paten with the bread and, holding it slightly raised above the altar, says inaudibly:

Blessed are you, Lord, God of all creation.
Through your goodness we have this bread to
    offer(3),
which earth has given and human hands have
    made(4).
It will become for us the bread of life.

Then he places the paten with the bread on the corporal.

If no offertory song is sung, the priest may say the preceding words in an audible voice; then the people may respond:

Blessed be God for ever.

The deacon (or the priest) pours wine and a little water into the chalice, saying inaudibly:

By the mystery of this water and wine may
  we come
to share in the divinity of Christ, who
    humbled himself
to share in our humanity.

Then the priest takes the chalice, and, holding it slightly raised above the altar, says inaudibly:

Blessed are you, Lord, God of all creation.
Through your goodness we have this wine to
    offer(3),
fruit of the vine and work of human hands(4).

(1) How do you participate as the altar is being prepared and the collection is being taken?

(2) How do you feel as you watch the gifts being presented?

(3) Are you aware of God's goodness through these gifts? If so, in what way?

(4) Do you experience a sense of human hands and work in these gifts? If so, how?

Reflection: Preparation of the Altar and the Gifts through Prayer over the Gifts (page 2)

It will become our spiritual drink.

Then he places the chalice on the corporal.

If no offertory song is sung, the priest may say the preceding words in an audible voice; then the people may respond:

Blessed be God for ever.

The priest bows and says inaudibly:

Lord, God, we ask you to receive us and be pleased with the sacrifice we offer you with humble and contrite hearts.

He may now incense the offerings and the altar. Afterwards the deacon or a minister incenses the priest and people.

Next the priest stands at the side of the altar and washes his hands, saying inaudibly:

Lord, wash away my iniquity; cleanse me
   from my sin.

Standing at the center of the altar, facing the people, he extends and then joins his hands, saying:

Pray, my brothers and sisters, that our
   sacrifice(5)
may be acceptable to God, the almighty
   Father.

The people respond:

May the Lord accept the sacrifice at your
   hands
for the praise and glory of his name,
for our good, and the good of all his Church(6).

PRAYER OVER THE GIFTS(7)

With hands extended, the priest sings or says the prayer over the gifts...

Lord,
make us worthy to celebrate these mysteries.
Each time we offer this memorial sacrifice,
the work of our redemption(8) is accomplished.
We ask this in the name of Jesus the Lord.

...at the end of which the people respond:

Amen.

(5) What does "sacrifice" mean to you?

(6) What does "Church" mean to you and how do you feel about that meaning?

(7) What are the gifts, as you perceive them?

(8) How do you respond to this "work of our redemption"?

Intent 2: Preparation of the Altar and the Gifts *through* Prayer over the Gifts

LITURGY OF THE EUCHARIST

PREPARATION OF THE ALTAR AND THE GIFTS(1)

After the liturgy of the word, the offertory song(2) is begun. Meanwhile the ministers place the corporal, the purificator, the chalice, and the missal on the altar.

It is desirable that the participation of the faithful be expressed by members of the congregation bringing up the bread and wine for the celebration of the eucharist or other gifts (3) for the needs of the Church and the poor.

The priest, standing at the altar, takes the paten with the bread and, holding it slightly raised above the altar, says inaudibly:

(4)Blessed are you, Lord, God of all creation.
Through your goodness we have this bread to
  offer,
which earth has given and human hands have
  made.
It will become for us the bread of life.

Then he places the paten with the bread on the corporal.

If no offertory song is sung, the priest may say the preceding words in an audible voice; then the people may respond:

Blessed be God for ever.

The deacon (or the priest) pours wine and a little water into the chalice, saying inaudibly:

By the mystery of this water and wine(5) may
  we come
to share in the divinity of Christ, who
  humbled himself
to share in our humanity.

Then the priest takes the chalice, and, holding it slightly raised above the altar, says inaudibly:

Blessed are you, Lord, God of all creation.
Through your goodness we have this wine to
  offer,
fruit of the vine and work of human hands.

(1) These gifts are the gifts of bread and wine, not yet Body and Blood of Christ. They symbolize our past, as we have taken God's raw materials and worked them with our hands. They symbolize the present in this now moment of preparation. Finally, they symbolize the future, as we look ahead to the time when they will become Jesus Christ once again.

(2) All song serves to unite the community. It gives spiritual meaning to bodily action.

(3) Bringing up the gifts is an external act. It not only signifies our concern for the Church and the poor (the monetary offering), but it also serves as the beginning of our concrete response to the Liturgy of the Word. In bringing up the gifts, we exercise our role as members of the priesthood of the faithful. Historically, it was a sign of mutual kinship when the head of the house received food from those who gathered in the house.

(4) Our response here, as above, is a response of praise. This prayer is modeled on the Jewish Berakah, a blessing prayer. Our culture is more familiar with addressing God with words and songs of thanks and praise rather than blessing God (why would God need our blessing?) because we tend to associate blessings with people and objects. Here we rejoice in and proclaim the blessedness of God.

(5) The mixing of water with the wine is symbolic of the human joined to the divine, first in the incarnate Christ and second through our participation and union with Christ (see Emminghaus 166; Johnson 73; Manly and Reinhard 275).

Intent 2: Preparation of the Altar and the Gifts through Prayer over the Gifts (page 2)

It will become our spiritual drink.

Then he places the chalice on the corporal.

If no offertory song is sung, the priest may say the preceding words in an audible voice; then the people may respond:

Blessed be God for ever.

The priest bows and says inaudibly:

Lord, God, we ask you to receive us and be pleased with the sacrifice we offer you with humble and contrite hearts(6).

He may now incense the offerings and the altar. Afterwards the deacon or a minister incenses the priest and people.

Next the priest stands at the side of the altar and washes his hands, saying inaudibly:

Lord, wash away my iniquity; cleanse me from my sin.

Standing at the center of the altar, facing the people, he extends and then joins his hands, saying:

Pray, my brothers and sisters, that our sacrifice
may be acceptable to God, the almighty Father.(7)

The people respond:

May the Lord accept the sacrifice at your hands
for the praise and glory of his name,
for our good and the good of all his Church(8).

PRAYER OVER THE GIFTS(9)

With hands extended, the priest sings or says the prayer over the gifts...

Lord,
make us worthy to celebrate these mysteries.
Each time we offer this memorial sacrifice,
the work of our redemption is accomplished.
We ask this in the name of Jesus the Lord.

...at the end of which the people respond:

Amen.

(6) This is a prayer of petition followed by a prayer of purification. The washing of the hands is symbolic of the desire to be cleansed within as well (GI 52; see also Johnson 75).

(7) This set of prayers is in the form of dialogue: the priest invites us to pray, and we respond and deepen the invitation by asking that the sacrifice be for all. To pray that our sacrifice be acceptable is to ask God to help us have a prayerful attitude: as we say yes to God, it must be with humble acceptance, thanks and praise.

(8) The "Church" is a powerful symbol that extends far beyond the organization with which we are so familiar. Most simply put, the Church is its members in the process of more fully becoming the Mystical Body of Christ. Church documents are eloquent when they speak of the Church, which is "the Lord's beloved Bride who calls to him and through him offers worship to the eternal Father" (CSL 7).

(9) This prayer ends the first part of the Liturgy of the Eucharist. It is a prayer of the day, which means that it changes with each celebration and addresses the focus of that particular Mass. This one is taken from the Mass of the Lord's Supper, and so refers to the redemption first offered in that supper.

Prayer of Acceptance

Presenter: Let us take a moment to pray now. (*Pause.*)

Heavenly Father and Mother,
loving presence in our lives,
you freely give us all that we have and possess.
We thank you for all you have given us.
Through your love and your grace,
help us to say "yes" to all that you have given us
with open hearts and minds.

Through your love and your grace,
we make ourselves a gift to you.
As we present ourselves to you,
receive us and be pleased with us.
Prepare us as individuals and as community
to become bearers of Christ to the world.
May we begin to serve you wholly according to your will.
We pray this through Jesus Christ, your son and our brother.

All: **Amen.**

Conclude with these or similar words:

Let us bow our heads and pause quietly
as we pray for the grace and love
to help us present ourselves to God
as individuals and as community.

Short silence before asking first person to come forward.

Session 5:
Preface *through* Memorial Acclamation

Rejoicing in God's presence in our lives,
we offer thanks and praise to the God who so loves us.

Schedule

Time	Description
5 minutes	Gathering Prayer
15 minutes	Reflection 1: Preface *through* Acclamation (Sanctus)
20 minutes	Group Process 1
10 minutes	Intent: Preface *through* Acclamation (Sanctus)
10 minutes	Break
15 minutes	Teaching: Eucharistic Prayer
15 minutes	Reflection 2: First Epiclesis *through* Memorial Acclamation
20 minutes	Group Process 2
30 minutes	Prayer with Plate and Cup
10 minutes	Group Process 3 (Optional)

Resource Sheets

Recommended Reading

◊ Valiquette, "What the Our Father Really Says," *St. Anthony Messenger* 92 (November 1976): 38-41.

Overview

This session moves us into the heart of the Liturgy of the Eucharist. The first reflection looks at the Preface; the second at Eucharistic Prayer I up to the Memorial Acclamation. We recommend that the second group process period be general discussion, simply for the sake of variety. A third (optional) group process period follows the Prayer with Plate and Cup. At the end of that prayer, you will need to determine whether or not people want to share their experience of the prayer. If not, dismiss the group early.

The session is fairly straightforward—the teaching involves a general overview and history of the eucharistic prayers; the intent looks at the Preface. For supplementary material on the Preface and eucharistic prayers, consider the following:

◊ Emminghaus, *Eucharist: Essence, Form, Celebration*, 168-189.

◊ Johnson, *Word & Eucharist Handbook*, 79-95.

◊ *General Instruction of the Roman Missal*, 54, 55, 108, 109.

◊ J. B. Ryan, "Eucharistic Prayers," *New Dictionary of Sacramental Worship*, 451-458.

◊ Ciferni and Hoffman, "The Eucharistic Prayer—Center and Summit?" *Liturgy 90* 23 (May/June 1992): 4-6, 15.

Gathering Prayer

See Session 2, page 54, for Gathering Prayer.

Reflection 1: Preface *through* Acclamation (Sanctus)

Distribute the reflection sheet, photocopied from page 122, to each participant.

Group Process 1

We recommend regular group sharing around the reflection questions.

Presenter's Reflection Questions

As you prepare for Session 5, you might ponder or bring to prayer the following questions:

◊ What is your own experience of the Eucharistic Prayer?

◊ When do you find it most meaningful to give thanks and praise?

◊ What helps you engage in the act of thanksgiving?

Dear God,
we give thanks
for places
of nature's truth
and freedom,
of joy,
inspiration and renewal,
places where
all creatures
may find acceptance
and belonging.
Let us search
for these places:
in the world,
in ourselves and
in others.

— Leunig,
Peace Prayers, 63

(Through the Memorial Acclamation) we support one another's faith in the paschal mystery, the central mystery of our belief. This acclamation is properly a memorial of the Lord's suffering and glorification, with an expression of faith in his coming.

— MCW 57

Intent: Preface *through* Acclamation (Sanctus)

Lead your discussion based on the intent sheet beginning on page 123.

Break

Teaching 1: Eucharistic Prayer

For this first teaching, you will not be looking at any specific liturgical text. The teaching will focus on the basic principles and history of the Eucharistic Prayer. We recommend addressing the following:

◊ History of the Eucharistic Prayer

◊ Overview of the four regular eucharistic prayers, the two for masses of reconciliation, and the three for masses with children

◊ Basic elements of the prayer: the thanksgiving, memorial, supplication and doxology

◊ Some basic vocabulary: epiclesis, anamnesis, berakah, memorial acclamation, anaphora, eucharist

Resources that cover these points are listed in the overview on the previous page.

During Session 6, you will present the entire text of Eucharistic Prayer I (the Roman Canon) section by section. Keep this week's discussion more general.

Reflection 2: First Epiclesis *through* Memorial Acclamation

Distribute the reflection sheet, photocopied from pages 125-127, to each participant.

Group Process 2

We recommend a group discussion at this point rather than a sharing that centers on the reflection questions, primarily because you have already experienced a personal sharing for this session and also because there is also opportunity to do more sharing at the end of the Prayer with Plate and Cup, which immediately follows this group process.

This particular Eucharistic Prayer touches upon many aspects of our faith life. The first reflection question opens up the experience of the Trinity; the fifth opens up the experience of what it means to be Church. With so much turmoil, questioning, and pain within the Catholic Church right now, these are good areas to address in a general discussion.

Questions you might consider for a group discussion include:

◊ What does the Trinity mean to you? Which person of the Trinity is the most accessible or real for you, and why?

◊ What does it mean to you to "be Church" right now? What makes it hard? What draws you in?

◊ What is your overall experience of the Eucharistic Prayer? What might help make it more meaningful?

Prayer with Plate and Cup

Introduction

This prayer is based upon Pierre Teilhard de Chardin's *Mass on the World*. To establish a meditative atmosphere and mood, begin with an antiphonal reading adapted from the Thanksgiving Day Preface (P 84). Then pray Teilhard de Chardin's prayer over the empty plate and cup. Pass the plate around the circle and invite each person to pray onto the plate their labors and fruits of the day. Next, pass the cup, this time inviting the participants to pray into the empty cup their suffering and pain. This prayer becomes an experience of feeling more intimately united with the joys and sorrows of Jesus and one another. Conclude by offering a prayer of blessing over each and singing a song.

Outline

1. Explain the prayer.

2. Begin with the Antiphonal Reading.

3. Say the offering prayer over plate and cup.

4. Pass plate and cup.

5. Say the blessing prayer over plate and cup.

6. Conclude with song. We recommend either "Song of the Body of Christ" by David Haas or "One Bread, One Body" by John Foley.

What distracts you the most when you are in church?

When the eucharistic prayers are said too quickly.

— A Participant

Come to me, all you who labor and are burdened, and I will give you rest. Take my yoke upon you and learn from me, for I am meek and humble of heart; and you will find rest for yourselves. For my yoke is easy, and my burden light.

— Matthew 11:28-30

Source of life and goodness, you have created all things, to fill your creatures with every blessing and lead all...to the joyful vision of your light.

— from Eucharistic Prayer IV

Presenter Preparation

Your own preparation for prayer should include the following:

◊ Make one copy of the Antiphonal Reading for each person.

◊ Bring a plate and cup, preferably earthenware (our bias is showing)

◊ Provide a small table; the one you are using for the candle, flowers, and liturgical objects each week may work, depending on its size.

◊ Prepare the words and/or a tape of the song you have chosen to close the prayer.

Details

We have incorporated the details of this prayer into the text of the prayer itself. The prayer takes place in your regular session space. Everything you need for this prayer follows, except for the Antiphonal Reading, of which each participant should have a copy.

Once you have concluded the Antiphonal Reading, proceed with the following, inviting each person to pray in his/her heart the words you are praying aloud.

Offering Prayer over Paten and Chalice

Since once again, Lord, I have neither bread, nor wine, nor altar, I will raise myself beyond these symbols, up to the pure majesty of the real itself; I will make the whole earth my altar and on it will offer you all the labours and sufferings of the world.

Lifting the empty paten, continue to pray:

I will place on my paten, O God, the harvest to be won by the renewal of labour.

Put the plate down and, lifting the empty cup, continue to pray:

What was the most moving part of the program for you and why?

Placing my works on the paten and my sufferings in the cup. This experience took me to my center.

— A Participant

Into my chalice I shall pour all the sap which is to be pressed out this day from the earth's fruits. My paten and my chalice are the depths of a soul laid widely open (Teilhard de Chardin 19).

Passing the Plate

Put the cup down and once again lift the plate, inviting each person to place upon the plate the labors of their lives. Decide whether you want them to do this in silence or out loud, or give them the choice. We have prayed both silently and out loud, and we have also allowed the participants to choose whichever is comfortable for them. All methods have worked well for us. (We prefer letting them choose). Pray your own labors and fruits upon the plate first so that they have a sense of what to do, then pass it to the person next to you. Once the plate has come full circle, place it lovingly back on the table. Again, keep in mind that if you are feeling the love, your body will express it and the group will notice.

Passing the Cup

In like manner pass the cup, inviting each person to pour into the cup the sufferings in their lives or in the world. Once the cup has come full circle, conclude with a prayer, holding the plate and the cup as you do so. A nice touch is to invite the people on either side of you to lift them as you say the prayer. You might also invite everyone to open lift their hands so that in some way they, too, are holding the plate and cup with you.

Closing Prayer

Generous God, we praise you for all that you have given to us. We place our joys and sufferings lovingly upon this plate and into this cup. We unite these joys and sufferings to those of Jesus and the whole church. We pray that your blessing wash over these gifts as gentle rain upon open soil. We pray that your spirit nourish these gifts and transform them into fruit for the world as Jesus nourishes and transforms us with his own body and blood. We ask this in Jesus' name. Amen.

Song

Conclude with singing either of the two songs mentioned in the Presenter Preparation.

Group Process 3

If there is time (we have allowed ten minutes or so), you might want to share how this prayer affected people. Again, you need to judge whether this would be helpful for them or not. If the mood of the group is contemplative and quiet, you might choose to close the session early.

This concludes Session 5.

...my cup overflows.
Only goodness and love
will pursue me
all the days of my life...
— Psalm 23:5-6

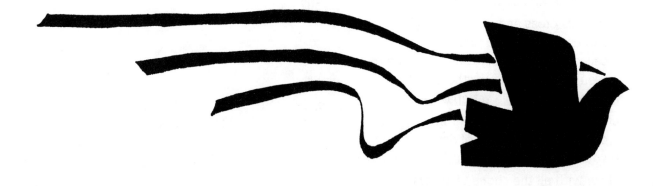

Session 5 Resource Sheets

Reflection 1: Preface *through* Acclamation (Sanctus)

PREFACE
Sundays in Ordinary Time I:
The Paschal Mystery and the People of God

Priest: The Lord be with you.

People: And also with you.

Priest: Lift up your hearts(1).

People: We lift them up to the Lord.

Priest: Let us(2) give thanks to the Lord our God.

People: It is right(3) to give him thanks and praise.

The priest continues the preface with hands extended.

Father, all-powerful and ever-living God,
we do well always and everywhere to give
     you thanks
through Jesus Christ our Lord.

Through his cross and resurrection(4)
he freed us from sin and death
and called us to the glory that has made us
a chosen race, a royal priesthood,(5)
a holy nation, a people set apart.

Everywhere we proclaim your mighty works
for you have called us out of darkness
into your own wonderful light(6).

And so, with all the choirs of angels(7) in
     heaven
we proclaim your glory
and join in their unending hymn of praise:

*At the end of the preface, he joins his hands
and, together with the people, concludes it by
singing or saying aloud:*

Holy, holy, holy Lord, God of power and
     might,
heaven and earth are full of your glory.
     Hosanna in the highest.
Blessed is he who comes in the name of the
     Lord.
     Hosanna in the highest.

(1) What does it mean to lift up your heart?

(2) Did you notice the switch in person from "you" to "us"? What does this signify for you?

(3) How does the word "right" speak to you?

(4) What do the cross and resurrection mean to you?

(5) Do you identify with the chosen race and royal priesthood? If so, how?

(6) When in your life has God called you out of darkness and into light? What happened?

(7) Do you experience a sense of joining in song with the choirs of angels? How do you feel about that?

Intent 1: Preface *through* Acclamation (Sanctus)

PREFACE
Sundays in Ordinary Time I:
The Paschal Mystery and the People of God(1)

Priest: The Lord be with you.

People: And also with you.(2)

Priest: Lift up your hearts.

People: We lift them up to the Lord.(3)

Priest: Let us give thanks to the Lord our God.

People: It is right to give him thanks and praise.(4)

Priest: Father,(5) all-powerful and ever-living God,
we do well always and everywhere to give you thanks
through Jesus Christ(6) our Lord.

(1) There are more than eighty prefaces from which to choose: prefaces for particular Sundays, holidays (including Thanksgiving and Independence Day) and special occasions (marriage, death, Christian unity). This particular preface (P 29) is used during Sundays in Ordinary Time and is taken in part from the first letter of Peter (1 Pt 2:9-10). The Preface begins with a solemn dialogue between the priest and the people that has three sets of proclamations (P) and responses (R). This dialogue leads the assembly into a deeper response with each set of P&Rs. This prayer format can affirm "the importance of the celebrating community at this time" (Empereur 156).

(2) This first set of P&Rs is a request by the priest and the people that the presence of the Lord be with each of them.

(3) In the second set of P&Rs, the priest asks the people to respond to that presence, and the people make an initial commitment.

(4) This third set of P&Rs joins the priest and people into one body with the word "us." We give God thanks for God's presence. The people affirm the call for thanksgiving.

(5) All of the eucharistic prayers are prayers of thanks and praise. They are always addressed to God the Father. These prayers should be prayed by one person: these are the prayers "in which the liturgical presidency has its clearest function" (Empereur 156). That said, it must also be noted that the Preface is a prayer in which "the *entire assembly* joins itself to Christ in acknowledging the great things God has done and in offering the sacrifice" (GI 54, my emphasis). The Preface expresses the thanksgiving most particularly. The thanks focus on the receiver of the gift (us) and the praise focuses on the giver of the gift (God). These prayers have a structure: an invitation-proclamation, a motivation (reason) for the thanks and praise, and a final invocation.

(6) *See next page.*

Intent 1: Preface (page 2)

(7)Through his cross and resurrection(8)
he freed us from sin and death
and called us to the glory that has made us
a chosen race, a royal priesthood,
a holy nation, a people set apart.

Everywhere we proclaim your mighty works
for you have called us out of darkness
into your own wonderful light.

And so, with all the choirs of angels in heaven
we proclaim your glory
and join in their unending hymn of praise:

Holy, holy, holy Lord, God of power and
    might,
heaven and earth are full of your glory.
    Hosanna in the highest.
Blessed is he who comes in the name of the
    Lord.
    Hosanna in the highest.(9)

(6) "Through Christ." Christ becomes our intercessor. At a very deep level we come to acknowledge that we are unable to give praise and thanks through our own power; this realization involves the beginning of self-surrender as we recognize our "radical dependence on the power of God" (Conn 7) (through Christ). This intercession appears throughout the eucharistic prayers, each time calling us more radically into self-surrender, not to be confused with or interpreted as self-negation.

(7) This part of the prayer contains the motivations (for the thanks and praise); in this Preface they center on the Paschal Mystery and the People of God. Rather than focusing on the exact content of these motivations, we should be "caught by wonder and awe and delight [of them] which leaves us inarticulate" (Manly and Reinhard 289).

(8) "Cross and Resurrection." Simply put, these images symbolize God's initiative and saving work in our lives: "the power to serve others is always God's free and justifying action" (Duffy 140). "O LORD, you mete out peace to us, for it is you who have accomplished all we have done" (Is 26:12). The cross and resurrection symbolize Jesus' self-gift "on account of others" (Duffy 145) and call us to deeper commitment and longing to give ourselves as Jesus gave to us.

(9) The praise is always sung when possible. This is a peak response and the conclusion of the preface (GI 55b). It was an early part of the eucharistic prayers, taken from synagogue morning service. "Hosanna" derives from the Hebrew word *Hoshiahnna*, "Pray, save [us]." Over time, it came to be less a plea for help and more a song of greeting and praise, as in Matthew's description of Jesus' entry into Jerusalem: "Hosanna to the Son of David;....hosanna in the highest" (21:9).

Reflection 2: First Epiclesis *through* Memorial Acclamation

EUCHARISTIC PRAYER I

In the first eucharistic prayer the words in brackets may be omitted. The priest, with hands extended, says:

We come to you, Father,(1)
with praise and thanksgiving,(2)
through Jesus Christ your Son.(1)

He joins his hands and, making the sign of the cross once over both bread and chalice, says:

Through him we ask you to accept and bless ✠
these gifts we offer you(3) in sacrifice.

With hands extended, he continues:

We offer them for your holy catholic Church,
watch over it, Lord, and guide it;
grant it peace and unity throughout the world.
We offer them for N. our Pope,
for N. our bishop,
and for all who hold and teach the catholic
　　faith
that comes to us from the apostles.(4)

Remember, Lord, your people,
especially those for whom we now pray, N.
　　and N.
Remember all of us gathered here before you.
You know how firmly we believe in you
and dedicate ourselves to you.
We offer you this sacrifice of praise
for ourselves and those who are dear to us.
We pray to you, our living and true God,
for our well-being and redemption.

In union with the whole Church(5)
we celebrate that day
when Jesus Christ, our Lord,
was betrayed for us.
We honor Mary,
the ever-virgin mother of Jesus Christ our
　　Lord and God.
We honor Joseph, her husband,
the apostles and martyrs
Peter and Paul, Andrew,
　　[James, John, Thomas,
　　James, Philip,

(1) What is it like for you to go to the Father through the Son?

(2) How do you think these two things — praise and thanksgiving — differ from each other?

(3) What is it like for you to offer gifts to the Father?

(4) Of these reasons that we offer these gifts, which one is the most meaningful to you and why? Do you have personal reasons why you offer gifts?

(5) Do you experience union with the whole Church. Why or why not?

Reflection 2: First Epiclesis through Memorial Acclamation (page 2)

Bartholomew, Matthew, Simon and Jude;
we honor Linus, Cletus, Clement, Sixtus,
Cornelius, Cyprian, Lawrence, Chrysogonus,
John and Paul, Cosmos and Damian]
and all the saints.
May their merits and prayers
gain us your constant help and protection.
    [Through Christ our Lord. Amen.]

With hands extended, he continues:

Father, accept this offering
from your whole family.
Grant us your peace in this life,
save us from final damnation,
and count us among those you have chosen(6).

He joins his hands.

    [Through Christ our Lord. Amen.]

With hands outstretched over the offerings, he says:

Bless and approve our offering;
make it acceptable to you,
an offering in spirit and in truth.
Let it become for us
the body and blood of Jesus Christ,
your only Son, our Lord.

He joins his hands.

    [Through Christ our Lord. Amen.]

The day before he suffered
to save us and all men,
that is today,
he took bread in his sacred hands
and looking up to heaven,
to you, his almighty Father,
he gave you thanks and praise.
He broke the bread,
gave it to his disciples, and said:

Take this, all of you, and eat it:(7)
this is my body which will be given up for you.

When supper was ended,
he took the cup.
Again he gave you thanks and praise,
gave the cup to his disciples, and said:

(6) How do you feel when you make this petition to the Father?

(7) These are words of command—"take and eat," "take and drink"—and inclusion—"all of you." What is it like to have Jesus saying these words to you?

Eucharist! © 1994 Resource Publications, Inc. All rights reserved.

Reflection 2: First Epiclesis through Memorial Acclamation (page 3)

Take this, all of you, and drink from it:(7)
this is the cup of my blood,
the blood of the new and everlasting covenant(8).
It will be shed for you and for all
so that sins may be forgiven.

Do this in memory of me.

Then [the priest sings or says:

Let us proclaim the mystery of faith:

[All respond:]

Dying you destroyed our death,
rising you restored our life.
Lord Jesus, come in glory.(9)

(8) Do you have a sense of belonging to this new covenant? What is that like?

(9) Can you put this mystery of faith in your own words?

Antiphonal Reading for Prayer with Paten and Chalice

Adapted from the Preface for Thanksgiving Day.

Presider: God of our past and our future,
gentle guide of the ever-present now,
it is our privilege and desire to join with all creation
in praising you, our wondrous God.

All: **You have made us in your own glorious image**
and set us in the midst of your creation.
You have done wondrous things for us!

Reader 1: In ages past, you chose a people and gave them a future full of promise.
When you freed them from oppression they brought with them the hope
that all people would be blessed and all people could be free.

All: **You have made us in your own glorious image**
and set us in the midst of your creation.
You have done wondrous things for us!

Reader 2: You have reached out to every generation
for all who have believed that Jesus, by his death and resurrection,
gave them a new freedom in the Spirit.

All: **You have made us in your own glorious image**
and set us in the midst of your creation.
You have done wondrous things for us!

Reader 1: You reached out to our ancestors
who came to this land out of a place of bondage and desolation
into a place of promise and hope.
You reach out to us in these days,
as you call us to share in your peace and work for your justice.

All: **You have made us in your own glorious image**
and set us in the midst of your creation.
You have done wondrous things for us!

Reader 2: And so when we pray with hearts full of love and gratitude,
we join with all our ancestors in faith
and all who have gone before us,
actively responding to your Word.

All: **You have made us in your own glorious image**
and set us in the midst of your creation.
You have done wondrous things for us!

Presider: May all that we do and all that we are
become a great hymn of praise and thanksgiving
for all you have done for us.

All: **Amen.**

Session 6:
Anamnesis *through* Sign of Peace

We remember God's gifts to us,
and trusting in God's mercy and love, we ask God's blessing.

Schedule

Time	Description
5 minutes	Gathering Prayer
15 minutes	Reflection: Anamnesis *through* Great Amen
20 minutes	Group Process 1
20 minutes	Intent 1: Eucharistic Prayer I
10 minutes	Break
10 minutes	Prayer 1: Dialogue Our Father
35 minutes	Prayer 2: Lord's Prayer and Peace Prayer
20 minutes	Group Process 2
15 minutes	Intent 2: Lord's Prayer *through* Sign of Peace

Resource Sheets

Recommended Reading

◊ Saliers, "Sanctifying Time, Place and People," *Weavings* 2 (September-October 1987): 18-28.

Overview

This session concludes the Eucharistic Prayer and looks at two of the preparation elements of the Communion Rite: the Lord's Prayer and the Sign of Peace. This session has one reflection period and two intent periods. The reflection period has seven questions. For the first intent period, you will walk your group through the entire Eucharistic Prayer I, introducing some new material and reinforcing what you taught during the last session. The second intent period covers the Lord's Prayer and Sign of Peace.

Preceding the prayer is a piece that we call the Dialogue Our Father. It is light-hearted and yet, through its gentle humor, it may easily create an impression that will long be remembered. Ask for a volunteer to help you with the dialogue. Ask for the volunteer just before the break and give him/her the copy of the dialogue in case he/she wants to review it before reading it aloud.

Prayer takes place in your prayer space/church around the altar and is followed by a time for group process, which focuses on the prayer. For supplementary material on the Lord's Prayer and the Sign of Peace, consider the following:

◊ Emminghaus, *Eucharist: Essence, Form, Celebration,* 190-194.

◊ Johnson, *Word & Eucharist Handbook,* 104-110.

◊ *General Instruction of the Roman Missal,* 56a,b, 111, 112.

◊ Woolfenden, "'Let us offer each other the sign of peace'—An Enquiry," *Worship* 67 (May 1993): 239-252.

Gathering Prayer

See Session 2, page 54, for Gathering Prayer.

Reflection 1: Anamnesis *through* Great Amen

Distribute the reflection sheet, photocopied from pages 140-141, to each participant.

Group Process 1

We recommend some form of regular group sharing based on the reflection questions.

Presenter's Reflection Questions

As you prepare for Session 6, you might ponder or bring to prayer the following questions:

◊ When, in your own life, has the act of remembering made the events feel as if they were happening right now?

◊ Think of the times when you have offered (or given) something to someone. What have your greatest joys been around the process? Your greatest fears?

◊ When you pray a familiar prayer like the "Our Father," what helps to make it meaningful rather than mindless?

◊ Meditate on the experience of peace for a while, inviting images, feelings or thoughts to arise.

Remember those who take part in this offering, those here present and all your people, and all who seek you with a sincere heart.

— from Eucharistic Prayer IV

Standing as the posture of the assembly for the eucharistic prayers has much more grounding in history than kneeling which entered the eucharistic liturgy when the communal action of giving thanks gave way to the adoration of the host.
— Ciferni and Hoffman 6

Intent 1: Eucharistic Prayer I

Begin by reviewing some of what you taught in Session 5. In particular, look at the general structure of the prayer, as described in the first item on the intent sheet for this session (page 142). Then walk the group through the prayer, using the explanation on the intent sheet, augmenting the material as you see the need.

Break

Prayer 1: Dialogue Our Father

Introduction

Before you begin, ask for a volunteer to play either "God" or "Human." If you can, put "God" behind a screen or just outside the room so that people only hear the voice; this is more fun but not necessary. I used this script in a workshop several years ago; recently, I ran into the man who played the human and he said he has never forgotten the experience. Because this prayer simply involves reading the dialogue, there is no Outline or Details.

Presenter Preparation

◊ Photocopy the Dialogue Our Father, pages 147-151, for both characters.

Prayer 2: Lord's Prayer and Peace Prayer

Introduction

This involves praying the "Our Father" in a participatory way. Immediately following that, there is a Scripture reading about peace, a sending forth of peace, and then the giving of peace to one another. The prayer takes place in your prayer/church space, so as soon as you are done with the Dialogue Our Father, proceed to the space. Your explanation about the prayer can take place there. We recommend forming a circle around the altar if there is enough room.

Outline

1. Process to prayer/church space.
2. Explain the prayer.
3. Pray the "Our Father."

4. Begin Sign of Peace with the Scripture Reading for Peace, a song, or your own prayer of peace.

5. Send peace.

6. Conclude with song, if desired.

Presenter Preparation

Your own preparation for prayer should include the following:

◊ Make sure you know where to pause for the "Our Father."

◊ Photocopy the Scripture Reading for Peace, page 152, which follows the Lord's Prayer. The number of photocopies you will need depends upon how you choose to do the reading (see page 136). Or, if you have a favorite prayer of peace, such as the Prayer of St. Francis ("Lord, make me an instrument of your peace"), bring a copy of that (obtaining permission to reprint first, if necessary).

◊ Provide words to and/or a tape of the song. We have used "Peace Is Flowing Like a River" by Cary Landry. Or you may choose, for example, Sebastian Temple's musical setting of the Prayer of St. Francis.

Details of Lord's Prayer

Begin with the words, "Our Father." As presenter, you will go first, putting that phrase into your own words. Pause, then invite each participant to put the phrase into his/her own words. Do not rush this prayer; plan to take a good twenty minutes with it. Allow silence to be as people encounter and enter their own inner space from which their words will come. This space has infinite depth, so there is nearly limitless room for expression. As the words begin to flow, one person's prayer will touch another's and stimulate more prayer. It will not be uncommon to have a person pray more than once during each phrase.

Your own pacing, patience and presence is influential; do not underestimate them. In your preparation for this, open yourself as completely as you can to the presence of God. As you lead the group through the process, people will move deeper and deeper into a profound interaction with God. The effect of all these people praying aloud from within is deeply moving.

Once you feel that no one has more to add to a particular part of the prayer, move on to the next phrase.

The following is an example of how this prayer might evolve. It is provided as an example to help you, as the presenter, have a better sense of the prayer. It is *not* meant to be distributed and read; each participant will speak from his/her heart.

I pray for a world where we live in partnership rather than domination; where "man's conquest of nature" is recognized as suicidal and sacrilegious; where power is no longer equated with the blade, but with the holy chalice: the ancient symbol of the power to give, nurture, enhance life. And I not only pray, but actively work, for the day when it will be so.
— Riane Eisler, *Peace Prayers*, 108

Then the wolf shall be a guest of the lamb, and the leopard shall lie down with the kid; The calf and the young lion shall browse together, with a little child to guide them.
— Isaiah 11:6

Our Father...

Our mother...Our creator...Our God who loves us so...My protector...Lord of all...Creator of all that is...Loving presence...The one who is everything in all of us...Gentle goodness...Beloved...The one who has made birds sing and flowers grow...You who watch over us and guide us...

...who art in heaven...

...who walks the earth with us...who is in the sea and in the air...who knows my every thought...who lives and breathes in me...who carries me when I fall...who cradles me lovingly when I am lonely...who is the light of my life...who shines upon me in my darkest moments...who is at once everywhere and in everything...

...hallowed be thy name...

...holy are you...blessed are you...blessed is the name of Jesus...all of creation calls you holy...help us to call you holy...help us to call you blessed...help us to know you more deeply as the most holy one...may we call upon your name always...may your name be forever on our lips and in our hearts...engrave your name upon my heart, O God...

...thy kingdom come...

...oh, loving Father, your kingdom is here among us...we long to be a part of your kingdom...we long for the time when there is peace among us...great is your kingdom...holy is your kingdom...may your kingdom come to rest in our hearts and minds...may we work toward birthing your kingdom...your kingdom is love and peace and harmony among all creatures...your kingdom is justice and equality and an end to war...we look forward to its day...we commit ourselves to bringing it about...

...thy will be done on earth as it is in heaven.

...dear God, may we come to know your heart's desire....may your will become our will....sometimes it is so difficult to know your will....your will is loving and kind and gentle....your will is firm and fair and just....your will is compassionate and tender....help us to know your will....help us to be less selfish....help us to embrace your will with our whole heart and our whole mind and our whole being.

Give us this day our daily bread...

Feed us, O Lord, and clothe us...Feed us with your love and your tenderness...Help us to want only what is necessary and no more...Help us to curb our materialistic desires...Nourish us with the body and blood of your Son...Nourished and fed, help us to become food for each other...Help us to be daily bread for one another...Help us to feed starving people...Help us to embrace their suffering...

...and forgive us our trespasses...

...forgive us, Father, for all that we have done wrong...help us to know when we have done wrong...help us to know when we have hurt someone else...help us to know when we have lied and cheated and been unkind...you are so merciful, O God...you are so forgiving...you so patiently wait for us to say we're sorry...you forgive us and forgive us and forgive us...

...as we forgive those who trespass against us...

...help us to be forgiving, dear Father...help us to turn the other cheek...sometimes it is so hard to be kind and loving...sometimes it is so hard to forgive...help us to follow your example, loving creator...help me to be less vindictive and petty...help me to be more accepting of others.

...and lead us not into temptation but deliver us from evil.

...you have saved us, Father....you guide us and you help us....you have given us Jesus' example to follow....protect us and never leave our side....save us from all the temptations we have in everyday life....show us the path to life, O God....help me not to lie so often—it is so easy for me to do and so hard to resist.

For thine is the kingdom and the power and the glory, now and forever, Amen.

Amen....So be it....You are so wonderful, dear God and Father....You are everything....Amen, amen, amen....My heart sings out to you, creator of the universe.

Once you have finished the prayer, allow a few minutes of silence before moving to the Peace Prayer.

Details of Peace Prayer

Once you have allowed several minutes of silence following the Lord's Prayer, move right into the Peace Prayer. The transition needs to be gentle and reverent. Your group is already in a contemplative place. You might begin by suggesting that, in preparation for the Peace Prayer, everyone meditate for a few moments on what "peace" means to them. Then proceed with the following.

> Come Lord! Change our lives, shatter our complacency. Make your word flesh of our flesh, blood of our blood and our life's purpose.
> — Dom Helder Camara, *Peace Prayers*, 80-81

Scripture Reading and/or Song

Begin with a reading from Scripture or a song that focuses on peace. The group could sing the song if they are familiar with it or simply listen to it on tape. If someone in your group is a cantor or a musician, you might ask him/her to help out.

The Scripture Reading for Peace might work well in place of the song or following it. You might read it aloud or give copies to each person and invite everyone read it silently.

Invitation to Silence

Once you finish the reading and/or song, invite each person to be silent and open on the inside and allow the peace of Christ to completely fill them. In the Sign of Peace, it is not our peace that we give but that of Christ. Allow several minutes of quiet around the altar for this to happen.

Sending Forth Christ's Peace to Those Who Are Not Here

Invite each person to send the peace forth to all those who are not present with you here and now. This is done in silence. Again, allow several minutes of quiet for each person to do this.

Offering Christ's Peace to Those Present

Finally, invite each person to give the peace of Christ to everyone who is present around the altar.

Group Process 2

Return to your regular session space, where you may want to do some group sharing around the prayer experience itself. Two variables will enter into your decision about having a group sharing now: time and desire. If the prayer took a long time, there may simply not be time to have a group process. If the prayer was particularly moving or deep for your participants, it may not "feel" appropriate to share now. As in previous sessions, judge the time and the mood.

You may want to use the following general questions:

◊ What was the overall experience like for you?

◊ What were you most aware of?

◊ What was most moving for you during the prayer?

◊ Were there awkward or uncomfortable moments for you? What caused them?

◊ How or what are you feeling right now?

Intent 2: Lord's Prayer *through* Sign of Peace

Lead your discussion based on the intent sheet beginning on page 153.

Before dismissing everyone, ask for a volunteer to bake a flat bread for the prayer in Session 7. See page 158 for details. The article by Robert Piercy, "Making Bread for Eucharist," includes a recipe for non-leavened bread.

Also in preparation for Session 7, find a priest and cantor for your celebration of Eucharist, which will take place in Session 8. See page 161 for details.

This concludes Session 6.

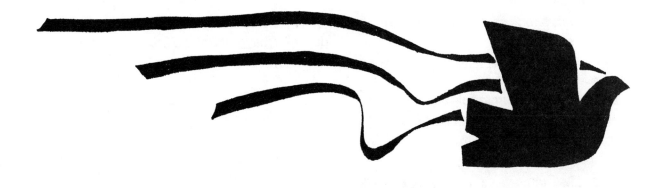

Session 6 Resource Sheets

Reflection 1: Anamnesis *through* Great Amen

Then, with hands extended, the priest says:

Father, we celebrate the memory of Christ(1),
    your Son.
We, your people and your ministers,
recall his passion,
his resurrection from the dead,
and his ascension into glory;
and from the many gifts you have given us
we offer to you, God of glory and majesty,
this holy and perfect sacrifice:
the bread of life
and the cup of eternal salvation.

Look with favor on these offerings
and accept them as once you accepted
the gifts of your servant Abel,
the sacrifice of Abraham, our father in faith,
and the bread and wine offered by your priest
    Melchisedech.

Bowing, with hands joined, he continues:

Almighty God,
we pray that your angel may take this sacrifice
to your altar in heaven.(2)
Then, as we receive from this altar
the sacred body and blood of your Son,

*He stands up straight and makes the sign of
the cross, saying:*

let us be filled with every grace and blessing.(3)

He joins his hands.

    [Through Christ our Lord. Amen.]

With hands extended, he says:

Remember, Lord, those who have died
and have gone before us marked with the
    sign of faith,
especially those for whom we now pray, N.
    and N.

*The priest prays for them briefly with joined
hands. Then, with hands extended, he
continues:*

May these, and all who sleep in Christ,
find in your presence(4)
light, happiness, and peace.

(1) What is it like for you to celebrate the memory of Christ?

(2) As you hear this prayer, do you mentally form any image or picture? What is it like?

(3) What particular grace and blessing do you desire? What grace and blessing have you experienced most strongly?

(4) When you hear this prayer, do you picture those who have died, especially anyone who is close to you, as sleeping in Christ and in the presence of the Father? What is that like for you?

Reflection 1: Anamnesis through Great Amen (page 2)

He joins his hands.

[Through Christ our Lord. Amen.]

With hands extended, he continues:

For ourselves, too, we ask
some share in the fellowship of your apostles
   and martyrs,
with John the Baptist, Stephen, Matthias,
   Barnabas,
   [Ignatius, Alexander, Marcellinus, Peter,
   Felicity, Perpetua, Agatha, Lucy,
   Agnes, Cecilia, Anastasia]
and all the saints.

The priest strikes his breast with the right hand, saying:

Though we are sinners,
we trust in your mercy and love(5).

With hands extended as before, he continues:

Do not consider what we truly deserve,
but grant us your forgiveness.

He joins his hands.

Through Christ our Lord.

He continues.

Through him you give us all these gifts.
You fill them with life and goodness,
you bless them and make them holy.

He takes the chalice and the paten with the host and, lifting them up, sings or says:(6)

Through him,
with him,
in him,
in the unity of the Holy Spirit,
all glory and honor is yours, almighty Father,
for ever and ever.

The people respond:

Amen(7).

(5) What helps or could help you trust in God's mercy and love in the face of your sin?

(6) What do you generally experience during the moment when the priest lifts up the chalice and paten?

(7) What is this "Amen" like for you? How does singing it differ from saying it?

Intent 1: Eucharistic Prayer I

In the *General Instruction of the Roman Missal,* we read, "Now the center and summit of the entire celebration begins: the eucharistic prayer, a prayer of thanksgiving and sanctification" (54).

The structure of the eucharistic prayers is fairly uniform and follows a set pattern:

◊ Thanksgiving, found predominantly in the Preface

◊ Acclamation, the "Holy, Holy, Holy" (Sanctus)

◊ Epiclesis, the invocation or calling down of the Holy Spirit

◊ Institution Narrative, which includes the Consecration

◊ Memorial Acclamation, of which there are four

◊ Anamnesis, an act of remembering

◊ Offering

◊ Intercessions

◊ Concluding Doxology

In the first eucharistic prayer the words in brackets may be omitted. The priest, with hands extended, says:

We come to you, Father,
with praise and thanksgiving,
through Jesus Christ your Son.

He joins his hands and, making the sign of the cross once over both bread and chalice, says:

Through him we ask you to accept and bless ✠ these gifts we offer you in sacrifice.(1)

With hands extended, he continues:

We offer(2) them for your holy catholic Church,
watch over it, Lord, and guide it;
grant it peace and unity throughout the world.
We offer them for N. our Pope,
for N. our bishop,
and for all who hold and teach the catholic faith
that comes to us from the apostles.

Eucharistic Prayer I is the Roman Canon. It is over 1,500 years old. It became a recognized prayer form during the rule of Pope Damasus I (366-384).

(1) This part of the Eucharistic Prayer is what Emminghaus calls a "transitional formula" (177). It serves to connect the Preface with the body of the Roman Canon. Although the gifts are blessed at this point, the epiclesis occurs much later in this particular eucharistic prayer.

(2) This prayer of offering is hierarchically ordered from church to pope to bishop to the general members of the church. This act of naming is part intercession, part remembrance, and serves to join all the faithful, both living and dead, into one Body.

                  Eucharist!

Intent 1: Eucharistic Prayer I (page 2)

Remember,(3) Lord, your people,
especially those for whom we now pray, N.
   and N.
Remember all of us gathered here before you.
You know how firmly we believe in you
and dedicate ourselves to you.
We offer you this sacrifice of praise
for ourselves and those who are dear to us.
We pray to you, our living and true God,
for our well-being and redemption.

(4)*In union with the whole Church
we celebrate that day
when Jesus Christ, our Lord,
was betrayed for us.
We honor Mary,
the ever-virgin mother of Jesus Christ our
   Lord and God.*
We honor Joseph, her husband,
the apostles and martyrs
Peter and Paul, Andrew,
   [James, John, Thomas,
   James, Philip,
   Bartholomew, Matthew, Simon and Jude;
   we honor Linus, Cletus, Clement, Sixtus,
   Cornelius, Cyprian, Lawrence, Chrysogonus,
   John and Paul, Cosmas and Damian]
and all the saints.
May their merits and prayers
gain us your constant help and protection.
   [Through Christ our Lord. Amen.]

With hands extended, he continues:

Father, accept this offering
from your whole family.
Grant us your peace in this life,
save us from final damnation,
and count us among those you have chosen.

He joins his hands.

   [Through Christ our Lord. Amen.]

With hands outstretched over the offerings, he says:

Bless and approve our offering;(5)
make it acceptable to you,(6)
an offering in spirit and in truth.

(3) In this prayer of remembering or "memorial prayer," in the Jewish sense of the act of remembering, we make all that we remember present now. This is a part of the mystery—how people and events that are not here and now can somehow be made present in a real way through this memorial prayer.

(4) Eucharistic Prayer I has six special forms for the portion of the prayer between the asterisks (*). This particular form is used on Holy Thursday.

(5) This is the first epiclesis. It is a prayer of petition, an appeal for the power of the Spirit to come and consecrate the gifts before us: transform the bread and wine into the Body and Blood of Christ and the assembly (who present themselves to God as well) into his mystical Body. In this particular Eucharistic Prayer, the invocation to the Holy Spirit is not explicit but implied; the other eucharistic prayers mention the Holy Spirit by name. By invoking the Holy Spirit, we acknowledge our own powerlessness to celebrate the Eucharist alone, to consecrate, to transform. We thus acknowledge the profound action of God in our lives.

(6) According to Manly and Reinhard in *The Art of Praying Liturgy*, this petition to make the offering acceptable is our way of asking God to help us with our own attitude during the offering. When we ask God to make the offering acceptable, we are saying to God, "Help us be thankful and filled with praise as we offer sacrifice, as we say 'yes' to your gifts to us, as we say 'yes' to the New Covenant you bring to us through Christ."

Intent 1: Eucharistic Prayer I (page 3)

Let it become for us
the body and blood of Jesus Christ,
your only Son, our Lord.

He joins his hands.

[Through Christ our Lord. Amen.]

(7)The day before he suffered
to save us and all men,
that is today,
he took bread in his sacred hands
and looking up to heaven,
to you, his almighty Father,
he gave you thanks and praise.
He broke the bread,
gave it to his disciples, and said:

(8)Take this, all of you, and eat it:
this is my body which will be given up for you.

When supper was ended,
he took the cup.
Again he gave you thanks and praise,
gave the cup to his disciples, and said:

(8)Take this, all of you, and drink from it:
this is the cup of my blood,
the blood of the new and everlasting covenant.
It will be shed for you and for all
so that sins may be forgiven.
Do this in memory of me.

Then [the priest] sings or says:

Let us proclaim the mystery of faith:

People with celebrant and concelebrants:

Dying you destroyed our death,
rising you restored our life.
Lord Jesus, come in glory.(9)

Then, with hands extended, the priest says:(10)

Father, we celebrate the memory of Christ,
   your Son.
We, your people and your ministers,
recall his passion,
his resurrection from the dead,
and his ascension into glory;
and from the many gifts you have given us
we offer to you, God of glory and majesty,
this holy and perfect sacrifice:

(7) This section of the Eucharistic Prayer is called the institution narrative, which includes the consecration. The whole Eucharistic Prayer (not just the institution narrative) reveals the mystery of Christ's death, resurrection and glorification. Prayed by the whole assembly (not just by the priest), this prayer makes Christ present to us in a very real way. Even though the prayer describes the breaking of the bread here, the actual breaking of bread occurs during the Communion Rite. The bread and wine may be incensed as a sign of reverence at the conclusion of the consecration.

(8) The words of Christ remain the same for all eucharistic prayers.

(9) The Memorial Acclamation has four forms; this is the third. All but the fourth form refer to the second coming of Christ. The Memorial Acclamation should be sung (MCW 54, 57). This act of singing gives us the opportunity as community to voice our thanks and praise to God for the gift of Christ in our midst. "[Christ] is present in the sacrifice of the Mass...especially under the eucharistic elements" (CSL 7).

(10) This section begins the anamnesis, which recalls Christ's passion, death, resurrection and ascension. Anamnesis, which comes from a Greek word for "memory," is far more than remembering. It is an action of making present now, in our midst, the saving action of Christ. This is not an easy concept to communicate or recognize because it has not been a part of our American culture.

Intent 1: Eucharistic Prayer I (page 4)

the bread of life
and the cup of eternal salvation.

Look with favor on these offerings(11)
and accept them as once you accepted
the gifts of your servant Abel,
the sacrifice of Abraham, our father in faith,
and the bread and wine offered by your priest
Melchisedech.

Bowing, with hands joined, he continues:

Almighty God,
we pray that your angel may take this sacrifice
to your altar in heaven.
Then, as we receive from this altar
the sacred body and blood of your Son,

*He stands up straight and makes the sign of
the cross, saying:*

let us be filled with every grace and blessing.(12)

He joins his hands.

[Through Christ our Lord. Amen.]

With hands extended, he says:

Remember, Lord, those who have died
and have gone before us marked with the
sign of faith,
especially those for whom we now pray, N.
   and N.(13)

*The priest prays for them briefly with joined
hands. Then, with hands extended, he
continues:*

May these, and all who sleep in Christ,
find in your presence
light, happiness, and peace.

He joins his hands.

[Through Christ our Lord. Amen.]

With hands extended, he continues:

For ourselves, too, we ask
some share in the fellowship of your apostles
   and martyrs,
with John the Baptist, Stephen, Matthias,
   Barnabas,
[Ignatius, Alexander, Marcellinus, Peter,

(11) This is the prayer of offering. "The Church's intention is that the faithful not only offer this victim but also learn to offer themselves and so to surrender themselves, through Christ the Mediator, to an ever more complete union with the Father and each other, so that at last God may be all in all" (GI 55f).

(12) This is the second epiclesis. Again, in this particular Eucharistic Prayer, the invocation to the Holy Spirit is not explicit but implied. It is a prayer that the Spirit come down now not only upon the gifts to make them the Body and Blood of Christ but also upon us as we join with these gifts to become the Body of Christ. "In the liturgy, by means of signs perceptible to the senses, human sanctification is signified and brought about in ways proper to each of these signs; in the liturgy the whole public worship is performed by the Mystical Body of Jesus Christ, that is, by the Head and his members" (CSL 7).

(13) These are the prayers of intercession, which "make it clear that the eucharist is celebrated in communion with the entire Church of heaven and earth" (GI 55g).

Intent 1: Eucharistic Prayer I (page 5)

Felicity, Perpetua, Agatha, Lucy,
  Agnes, Cecilia, Anastasia]
and all the saints.

The priest strikes his breast with the right hand, saying:

Though we are sinners,
we trust in your mercy and love.

With hands extended as before, he continues:

Do not consider what we truly deserve,
but grant us your forgiveness.

He joins his hands.

Through Christ our Lord.

He continues.

Through him you give us all these gifts.
You fill them with life and goodness,
you bless them and make them holy.

He takes the chalice and the paten with the host and, lifting them up, sings or says:

Through him,
with him,
in him,
in the unity of the Holy Spirit,
all glory and honor is yours, almighty Father,
for ever and ever.(14)

The people respond:

Amen.(15)

(14) This is the concluding doxology, which is a praise of God—all glory and honor be yours! Pay special attention to the words "through," "with" and "in" Jesus. These words lead us from a sense of Jesus as intercessor ("through") to Jesus as companion ("with") to Jesus as an experience of union ("in"). Each sense leads us a little bit deeper into our experience of God. These three words summarize succinctly the entire Eucharistic Prayer.

(15) This is the Great Amen. It is our final *yes* to the entire Eucharistic Prayer. Begin to understand all that the Eucharistic Prayer says, all that we say amen to. We must begin to feel this Amen to the depth of our being, with feeling and resonance. We have heard and said several "Amens" leading up to this one; often they just emerge from our mouths without any intention on our part at all. Let the walls of the church vibrate with this Amen; let the people who surround us feel the force of our response so that it becomes a unified, single voice from the Body of Christ, crying out to God the Father, "Yes, oh yes!"

Dialogue Our Father

When God Speaks: Praying the "Our Father" in a Relational Way *(adapted from a work by Dwight Vogel)*

Human:	**Our Father who art in heaven—**
God:	Yes?
Human:	*(Automatically)* Don't interrupt me, I'm praying.
God:	But you called me.
Human:	Called you? I didn't call you. I'm praying. If you continue to interrupt me, this could take forever and I have a lot to do today. **Our Father who art in heaven—**
God:	There, you did it again!
Human:	Did what?
God:	You called me. You said, "Our Father who art in heaven." So, here I am. I'm answering you. What's on your mind?
Human:	*(Stumbling a little)* Oh, boy, well, um, I really didn't mean anything by it, you know, by calling you. I was just saying my prayers for the day. This is just part of my morning routine. I always say the Lord's Prayer. It makes me feel good, kind of like doing one of my daily chores.
God:	Well, OK, you can go on.
Human:	**Hallowed be thy name—**
God:	Stop there for just a minute, please. What do you mean by "hallowed?"
Human:	By what?
God:	By "hallowed be thy name."
Human:	It means, well, um...I don't know what it means. I just say it every day. How should I know what it means? It's just part of the prayer. But now you've made me curious. What does it mean?
God:	It means holy, sacred, respected.
Human:	Knowing that somehow changes the way how I feel about saying those words. I just never thought about it before this. **Thy kingdom come, thy will be done on earth as it is in heaven.**
God:	Do you really mean that?
Human:	*(A little annoyed)* Now what? You really do keep interrupting me! Do I really mean what?

Dialogue Our Father (page 2)

God: What you just said: "Thy kingdom come, thy will be done on earth as it is in heaven."

Human: I wouldn't say it if I didn't mean it!

God: So, what are you doing about it?

Human: Doing? I don't suppose I'm doing anything, but I do think it would be so much easier, better, really, if you just took control of everything down here like you have up there.

God: Let's be a little more specific. Does my will guide you?

Human: (*Defensively*) Well, I'm praying right now, aren't I? And I do go to church.

God: That's not what I asked you. Who is really in control here? Do you come to me when you make decisions? Have you let me into your life? Do you let me truly be your Lord?

Human: Oh, come on, I think you're getting awfully picky. I'm not all that bad. In fact, I'm pretty good. I try to do what I'm supposed to do.

God: Excuse me, I heard you pray for my will to be done. If that is going to happen, it will have to start with the ones who are praying for it, like you, for example.

Human: (*Thoughtfully*) I guess when you put it that way...when you put it that way, I have to admit that I'm not very dependent on you. I do like to be in control of my own life. In fact, I work very hard at doing that.

God: Yes, I must admit, I've noticed.

Human: I haven't thought about it until now, but I really would like to let you take some more control of my life. If I gave you some of that control, I wouldn't have to work so hard. I'd probably feel more free!

God: It feels like we are getting somewhere now. It sounds as though we could begin working together, you and I.

Human: You're right, but look, like I said before, I've got lots to do today. I really just need to finish this part of my routine.

God: Go ahead then.

Human: **Give us this day our daily bread.**

God: I do each day in the Eucharist. All you need to do is come and pray and come and eat.

Human: Come and pray and come and eat?

Dialogue Our Father (page 3)

God: Praying is a dangerous thing. You could wind up changed, you know. That's what I've been trying to point out to you this morning. You called me, and here I am. It's too late to stop now. Keep on praying. I'm interested in the next part of your prayer. (*Pause*) Well, go on.

Human: (*Hesitating*) I'm not sure I want to pray the next part.

God: Why not?

Human: I'm scared! Look at what's gone on between us already. I know what you're going to say next.

God: Just try me and see.

Human: **Forgive us our trespasses as we forgive those who trespass against us.**

God: What about your friend Bill?

Human: See, I knew it! I just knew that's what you were going to say next! Look, you know all about Bill. He cheated me out of some money and as soon as my back was turned, he lied about me. I trusted him and he betrayed me!

God: But what about your prayer: "as we forgive those who trespass against us?"

Human: (*Exasperated*) Oh, come on! There are just some things that can't be forgiven. Do you know how good it has made me feel just to dream about bad things happening to that creep?

God: (*Gently*) It can't feel that good to be so bitter and vengeful.

Human: Don't be so sure about that! I'm not planning on doing something really bad back to him, just a little something that will teach him a lesson, something that will make him sorry he ever did those things to me!

God: That won't make you feel better. Trust me. Somewhere inside of you, you'll just feel worse. Hatred and vengeance just breed more hatred and vengeance. But I can help you, if you'll let me.

Human: How?

God: Forgive Bill. As I forgive you. Then the hatred and the vengeance and the sin will no longer be yours. You'll feel a lot more free and a lot more peaceful.

Human: Easy for you to say! You're asking an awful lot. I can't forgive that...that jerk, just like that! I mean, do you know all the things he's done to me, how much he's hurt me—

Dialogue Our Father (page 4)

God: (*Interrupting*) Now, hold on, just for a minute. If you are unable to forgive him, if you stay this stuck, it's difficult for me to forgive you. It's that simple. If you will just allow yourself to be open to my grace, it will not feel so impossible.

Human: (*Feeling some release*) Oh, I know you're right. This need to get even really has begun to feel pretty heavy. And I do want you to forgive me. I know Bill has got to feel lousy that he did those things to me. He must be pretty stuck, too. When I look at things that way, I do begin to feel forgiveness. Maybe I even want to ask you to help him, too.

God: You've just said a lot! How does it feel?

Human: Wow! I'm surprised. I've been stuck on this Bill thing for a long time. I feel a whole lot lighter. You know, I even think that maybe I won't go to bed so uptight tonight with my stomach all in knots. This has been a pretty big thing in my life for a while now.

God: Why don't you continue with your prayer now?

Human: **And lead us not into temptation, but deliver us from evil.**

God: There. I can do that. I can protect you, but you have to help, too. Like not putting yourself in a place where you know you will be tempted.

Human: What do you mean by that?

God: You know yourself that some of your friends—your so-called "friends"—have been trying to persuade you to do things that aren't so great. I know you've been struggling with that. Before long, they'll have you involved in all the wrong things.

Human: I don't understand.

God: Oh, I think you do. You've done it before. You've been caught in a bad situation, you've gotten in trouble and then you've come running to me saying, "Please help me out of this, God. I promise I'll never, ever do it again!"

Human: Ohhh, this does sound familiar. I'm so ashamed, I'm so sorry.

God: But you can make changes now, changes that will help you to avoid these situations. And I will help you. Why don't you go on?

Human: **For thine is the kingdom and the power and the glory, forever and ever amen.**

God: Do you know what would bring me glory? Have you ever thought about it? What might make me really happy?

Dialogue Our Father (page 5)

Human: I'm not sure. I feel confused a lot of the time. But I do want to know! I do want to have a deeper relationship with you. I mean, I don't say it very often, but there is a desire to be with you that just never goes away.

God: You've just answered my question!

Human: I did?

God: Yes! It really is so simple. What will bring me glory, what will make me truly happy, is just to have people like you truly love me and to have people like you let me love them. It has been wonderful to be with you this morning!

Scripture Reading for Peace

Adapted from Ephesians 2:13-18 and John 14:27.

But now in Christ Jesus you who once were far off
have been brought near through the blood of Christ.

It is he who is our peace,
and who made the two of us one
by breaking down the barrier of hostility that kept us apart.

In his own flesh,
he abolished the law
with its commands and precepts
to create in himself one new person
from us who had been two
and to make peace, reconciling all of us to God
in one body through his cross,
which put that enmity to death.

He came and announced
the good news of peace to you who were far off,
and to those who were near;
through him, we both have access in one Spirit to the Father.

And Jesus said to his disciples:

Peace is my farewell to you,
my peace is my gift to you;
I do not give it to you as the world gives peace.
Do not be distressed or fearful.

Intent 2: Lord's Prayer *through* Sign of Peace

COMMUNION RITE(1)

LORD'S PRAYER(2)

*The priest...with hands joined sings or says
...the following:*

Let us pray with confidence
to the Father in the words our Savior gave us.

*He extends his hands and he continues, with
the people:*

Our Father, who art in heaven,
hallowed by thy name;
thy kingdom come; thy will be done
on earth as it is in heaven.(3)
Give us this day our daily bread;
and forgive us our trespasses
as we forgive those who trespass against us;
and lead us not into temptation,(4)
but deliver us from evil.

*With hands extended, the priest continues
alone:*

Deliver us, Lord,
from every evil,
and grant us peace in our day.
In your mercy keep us free from sin
and protect us from all anxiety
as we wait in joyful hope
for the coming of our Savior, Jesus Christ.(5)

He joins his hands.

DOXOLOGY

*The people end the prayer with the
acclamation:*

For the kingdom,
the power and the glory are yours,
now and for ever.(6)

(1) The Communion Rite begins with a rite of preparation, much like the Introductory Rites prepare us to hear the Word and the Preparation Rites at the altar prepare the gifts and us for the Eucharistic Prayer. The first part of this rite prepares us for the actual meal, the banquet. The rite should flow easily and the moment should not create a division between Jesus' words at the consecration to take and eat and the actual moment when we do take and eat.

(2) The Lord's Prayer comes to us from the Gospels. This centuries-old prayer can be said to sum up all that we believe and hope for. It consists of an address—"Our Father"—and two sets of petitions.

(3) The first set of petitions focuses on the action of God as Father and the coming of God's kingdom.

(4) The second set of petitions focuses on our needs and fears as they are met by the action of God. Our petition for daily bread is often misunderstood. It is not simply a literal plea for food; it refers primarily to the coming banquet in the kingdom of God. It also refers to the Eucharist—to our willingness to share in the suffering and to our commitment to bringing about the unity that we celebrate in the one broken and shared bread.

(5) This is properly called the "embolism" and is "said by the principal celebrant alone, with hands outstretched" (GI 193). It is a petition for peace and freedom from sin and disharmony.

(6) This is our acclamation. Let it be joyful and strong, full of the praise for all of God's action in our lives.

Intent 2: Lord's Prayer through Sign of Peace (page 2)

SIGN OF PEACE(7)

Then the priest, with hands extended, says aloud:

Lord Jesus Christ, you said to your apostles:
I leave you peace, my peace I give you.
Look not on our sins, but on the faith of your
    Church,
and grant us the peace and unity of your
    kingdom

He joins his hands.

where you live for ever and ever.

The people answer:

Amen.

The priest, extending and joining his hands, adds:

The peace of the Lord be with you always.

The people answer:

And also with you.

Then the deacon (or the priest) may add:

Let us offer each other the sign of peace.

All make an appropriate sign of peace, according to local custom.

(7) The priest's first words of the Sign of Peace are based on John 14:27. The words, which address Jesus, comprise the first public prayer addressed to Jesus. Up until this point, all the prayers of the liturgy have been addressed to the Father. "As a preparation for the communion, it is an expression and experience of faith...an expression of the experience of sharing Christ's life and prayer here and now" (Manly and Reinhard 300).

Session 7:
Breaking of the Bread *through* Dismissal

Christ's body and blood nourish us,
and we are sent forth to nourish and feed others.

Schedule

Time	Description
5 minutes	Gathering Prayer
10 minutes	Reflection 1: Breaking of the Bread *through* Prayer after Communion
10 minutes	Group Process 1
30 minutes	Prayer: Taking, Blessing and Breaking of Bread
10 minutes	Intent 1: Breaking of the Bread *through* Prayer after Communion
10 minutes	Break
10 minutes	Reflection 2: Concluding Rite
10 minutes	Group Process 2
10 minutes	Intent 2: Concluding Rite
30 minutes	Preparation for Session 8: Liturgy and Agape
15 minutes	Program Evaluation

Resource Sheets

Recommended Reading

◊ Piercy, "Making Bread for Eucharist," *Liturgy 90* 23 (February/March 1992): 4-5.

◊ Gentry-Akin, "To Make Eucharist Is To Give Thanks," *Creation* 5 (January-February 1989): 42-43.

◊ Jorgensen, "The Dismissal Rite: A Blessing for Action," *Modern Liturgy* 19 (October 1992): 18-21.

Overview

This session has two reflection periods and two intent periods. The first reflection period has seven questions; the second has six. The intent portions of the session are short—ten minutes each—and fairly straightforward. The prayer is a gentle piece that takes place in your regular space. For supplementary material on this portion of the Communion Rite and the Concluding Rite, consider the following:

◊ Emminghaus, *Eucharist: Essence, Form, Celebration,* 194-211.

◊ Johnson, *The Word & Eucharist Handbook,* 110-139.

◊ *General Instruction of the Roman Missal,* 56c-k, 57, 113-125, 240-242, 281-286, 293.

◊ *Appendix to the General Instruction,* 240, 242.

◊ *Environment and Art in Catholic Worship,* 96.

◊ *Music in Catholic Worship,* 48-49, 62, 68, 72-73.

◊ *Liturgical Music Today,* 20.

During this session, make all the preparations for the celebration of Eucharist that concludes the program. You will need a Sacramentary and a Lectionary for these preparations. The provided checklist and preparation sheet will help you in this task. In addition to preparing for the Eucharist, plan for your agape meal: what type of food and who will bring what, including utensils, paper goods, etc.

There is also time this week to fill out program evaluations; it is much better to have participants fill them out during the session rather than take them home (your rate of completion and return will be much better!).

Gathering Prayer

See Session 2, page 54, for Gathering Prayer.

Reflection 1: Breaking of the Bread *through* Prayer after Communion

Distribute the reflection sheet, photocopied from pages 164-166, to each participant.

Presenter's Reflection Questions

As you prepare for Session 7, you might ponder or bring to prayer the following questions:

◊ What does the breaking of bread mean to you in a ritual sense? In your daily life?

◊ When do the ritual and daily experiences of breaking bread intersect and/or complement each other in your life?

◊ How has your experience of receiving Eucharist changed and developed over the last few years?

◊ What does it mean to you to love and serve? What are the elements of healthy love and service?

◊ What draws you into deeper love and service?

> (T)he renewal in the eucharist of the covenant between the Lord and his people draws the faithful into the compelling love of Christ and sets them on fire.
> — CSL 10

Group Process 1

We recommend regular group sharing around the reflection questions.

Prayer: Taking, Blessing and Breaking of Bread

Introduction

This prayer is based on Jesus' action of taking bread, blessing it and breaking it. In the liturgy, these are actions in which, as celebrants, we join with the priest in mind, heart and spirit; unless we are communion ministers, we do not usually experience the actual breaking of the bread during the Communion Rite. This prayer gives you the chance to enter into the actual experience not only with mind, heart and spirit, but with body as well. This prayer is not a consecration; it is simply an engagement with a long-standing tradition of taking, blessing and breaking, modeled on the Jewish form of blessing, the berakah. The blessing includes praise, thanksgiving and petition.

Outline

1. Pass the bread around the circle, inviting each person to simply take the bread in his/her hands.

2. Pass the bread around the circle a second time, inviting each person to bless the bread, either in silence or aloud.

3. Pass the bread around the circle a third time, inviting each person to break the bread.

Presenter Preparation

Your own preparation for prayer should include the following:

◊ Bring a large plate and one large, flat bread. Even if someone volunteered in Session 6 to bake it, bring a contingency loaf.

Details

The Taking of Bread

These actions of taking, blessing and breaking are contemplative. In the action of taking, invite each person to do so with all of his/her awareness. You may introduce the action of taking by asking the participants to remember times in their lives when bread has been significant, times when they have taken bread into their own hands. In the mystery of the Eucharist, we are united together through all of time with all other people who have taken bread into their hands. You may talk of the significance of bread in our daily lives. You may invite them to remember images of wheat—single grains of wheat, stalks of wheat gracefully yielding to gentle breezes, expansive fields of wheat, stretching before you for as far as the eye can see. You may invite them to think of the process of grinding the grain, of refining the resulting flour by separating the endosperm from the bran and germ. You may invite them to think about the process of making bread, "which earth has given and human hands have made." You may ask them to be aware of the feel of the bread, the smell of the bread as they take it into their own hands. Your introduction serves the purpose of stimulating their imaginations and memories.

Once you have introduced the prayer, take the bread into your own hands and hold it prayerfully for a minute or so, just being present to the action of taking the bread. Then, pass the plate to the person next to you.

The Blessing of Bread

When the plate has come full circle, invite each person to bless the bread. The blessing may be silent or aloud, whichever way each person is comfortable. In the action of blessing, you engage in an act of praise for all that God is, an act of thanks for all that God has done, an invocation or intercession that God will continue to bless you and take care of you. Take the bread into your hands once again and pray aloud the first blessing.

The Breaking of Bread

Again, when the plate has come full circle, invite each person to break the bread in silence as Jesus himself broke bread. In the action of breaking, you engage in a process that has many levels, both literal and symbolic. Invite them to feel the bread yield to the motion of their hands. Invite them to remember times when they have given of themselves to others. Invite them to remember that we all experience brokenness in our own lives, that God invites us to be broken for each other, as Christ was broken for us. In the act of breaking, we take part in each other's lives in a way that brings us into union with one another.

Thanksgiving

When the plate has come full circle once again, reverently place the bread on your small prayer table. Invite each person to give thanks to God in their hearts and in their own way for the acts of taking, blessing and breaking.

The action of the breaking of the bread, the simple term for the eucharist in apostolic times, will more clearly bring out the force and meaning of the sign of the unity of all in the one bread and of their charity, since the one bread is being distributed among the members of one family.

— GI 283

While they were at supper, (Jesus) took bread, said the blessing, broke the bread, and gave it to his disciples.
— from Eucharistic Prayer IV

Reflection and Sharing

Then, invite everyone to turn to the person on his/her right or left and share a thought or reflection about what was most significant about this prayer.

During the break, you might invite each person to eat a piece of the bread if they would like.

Intent 1: Breaking of the Bread *through* Prayer after Communion

Lead your discussion based on the intent sheet beginning on page 167.

Break

Reflection 2: Concluding Rite

Distribute the reflection sheet, photocopied from pages 170-171, to each participant.

Group Process 2

We recommend a group discussion that focuses on the "sending forth." Reflection questions to consider include:

◊ How does liturgy prepare you to go forth to "love and serve the Lord?"

◊ How do you bring your experience of liturgy out into the world?

◊ How do you connect liturgy and social justice in your own worshiping community? In your family? In your workplace? In your town or city?

Go, therefore, and make disciples of all the nations...teaching them to observe all that I have commanded you. And behold, I am with you always, until the end of the age.
— Matthew 28:19-20

Intent 2: Concluding Rite

Lead your discussion based on the intent sheet beginning on page 172.

Preparation for Session 8: Liturgy and Agape

Following Intent 2, you have approximately thirty minutes to prepare for the Session 8 liturgy. This is an excellent opportunity for everyone to put into practice what they have learned and experienced over the course of the program.

What do you need to do? *Prior to this session*, find a priest and a cantor so that they can be a part of the preparations for the liturgy, if they choose to do so. Look to your group first. Do you have cantors or priests in the group? If so, your task will be easy. If not, ask the members of your group if they know someone willing to be a cantor and a priest.

Second, make sure you bring a Sacramentary, Lectionary, and resources for music. Now you are ready to begin the preparations.

Make enough photocopies of the checklist and preparation sheet (pages 174 and 175) for the group. Distribute them when you are ready to begin this part of the session. As you make decisions based on the checklist, write the information on the Liturgy Preparation Sheet.

The group as a whole should accomplish the following:

◊ Decide on the Scriptures. You might want to use the Scriptures of the day or the Scriptures specified in the Lectionary for certain "Masses and Prayers for Various Needs and Occasions"or "Votive Masses." You might especially consider choosing "For Unity of Christians," "For Peace and Justice," "For Any Need," "In Thanksgiving," or "Holy Spirit." Refer to *General Instruction*, chapter 8, section I, "Masses and Prayer for Various Needs and Occasions," for more information about these masses.

◊ Once the texts are picked, suggest that everyone pray with them throughout the week in anticipation of the liturgy.

◊ Based on the Scriptures, pick appropriate music, selections that are familiar and meaningful to your group (see checklist for details).

◊ Pick volunteers for the various roles and tasks involved in the celebration (see checklist for details).

◊ Decide what type of meal you want to have. Do you want simple hors d'oeuvres, a full evening meal, brunch, a continental-type breakfast, or coffee and dessert? Your

---

Like the covenant itself, the liturgical celebrations of the faith community (Church) involve the whole person. They are not...merely rational and intellectual exercises, but also human experiences calling on all human faculties: body, mind, senses, imagination, emotions, memory. Attention to these is one of the urgent needs of contemporary liturgical renewal.

— EACW 5

The sacred scriptures ought to be the source and inspiration of sound planning for it is of the very nature of celebration that people hear the saving words and works of the Lord and then respond in meaningful signs and symbols.

— MCW 11

The pastoral effectiveness of a celebration will be heightened if the texts of readings, prayers, and songs correspond as closely as possible to the needs, religious dispositions, and aptitude of the participants.

— GI 313

The acclamations (gospel acclamation, doxology after the Lord's Prayer, and eucharistic acclamations...) are the preeminent sung prayers of eucharistic liturgy. Singing these acclamations makes their prayer all the more effective.

— LMT 17

choice will probably depend, in large part, on the time of your liturgy. Once the basic type of meal has been chosen, let the small group take care of the details.

Allow fifteen minutes for the above, then divide the group into three smaller groups, which should accomplish the following:

◊ Group One writes the General Intercessions.

◊ Group Two chooses the appropriate liturgical texts. Plan on being a part of this group, as their task is the most involved and technical, and your expertise will help them. For assistance, refer to General Instruction, chapter 7, "Choice of the Mass and Its Parts," 318-324.

◊ Group Three plans the meal you have chosen. They need to assess the facility where you will have the meal, make a list of who will bring what, making sure that they include paper goods and drinks.

Allow fifteen minutes for the above, then call the group back together and invite them to bring to Session 8 some symbol of either themselves or their experience of the program. The group might have questions around this. Answer them thoughtfully until you sense that everyone understands what you are asking. You may use these symbols for the reflection period that precedes the liturgy, and we suggest that each person place his/her symbol in front of the altar during the celebration.

To complete preparations, make sure that the priest and the cantor each have a copy of the Liturgy Preparation Sheet. Make notes of what needs to be copied (music, etc., obtaining permission to reprint first, of course) for the assembly's full participation in the liturgy (we tend to be minimalists in this area, so we advise that less is better).

Program Evaluation

Finally, proceed to the program evaluation. You may want to play quiet instrumental music while the participants fill it out.

Immediately before closing the session, remind participants to bring their symbol to Session 8.

This concludes Session 7.

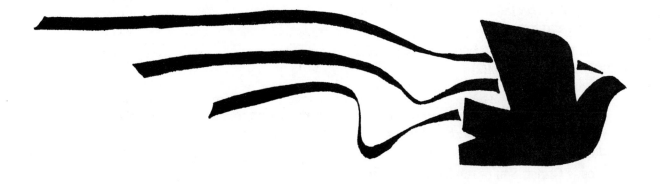

Session 7 Resource Sheets

Reflection 1:
Breaking of the Bread *through* Prayer after Communion

BREAKING OF THE BREAD

Then the following is sung or said:

(1)Lamb of God, you take away the sins of the
> world:
> have mercy on us.
Lamb of God, you take away the sins of the
> world:
> have mercy on us.
Lamb of God, you take away the sins of the
> world:
> grant us peace.

*[The "Lamb of God"] may be repeated until
the breaking of the bread is finished, but the
last phrase is always "Grant us peace."*

*Meanwhile, he takes the host and breaks it
over the paten. He places a small piece in the
chalice, saying inaudibly:*

May this mingling of the body and blood of
> our Lord Jesus Christ(2)
bring eternal life to us who receive it.

PRIVATE PREPARATION OF THE PRIEST

*Then the priest joins his hands and says
inaudibly:*

Lord Jesus Christ, Son of the living God, by
the will of the Father and the work of the Holy
Spirit your death brought life to the world. By
your holy body and blood free me from all my
sins, and from every evil. Keep me faithful to
your teaching, and never let me be parted
from you.

COMMUNION

*The priest genuflects. Taking the host, he
raises it slightly over the paten and, facing the
people, says aloud:*

This is the Lamb of God
who takes away the sins of the world.
Happy are those who are called to his
> supper.(3)

He adds, once only, with the people:

(1) What is it like for you when you say or sing
these words?

(2) Are you aware of this action and prayer? If
so, what meaning does it hold for you?

(3) Do you feel personally called to his supper?
What is that like for you?

     Eucharist!

Reflection 1: Breaking of the Bread through Prayer after Communion (page 2)

Lord, I am not worthy to receive you,
but only say the word and I shall be healed.(4)

Facing the altar, the priest says inaudibly:

May the body of Christ bring me to
everlasting life.

*He reverently consumes the body of Christ.
Then he takes the chalice and says inaudibly:*

May the blood of Christ bring me to
everlasting life.

He reverently drinks the blood of Christ.

*After this, he takes the paten or other vessel
and goes to the communicants. He takes a
host for each one, raises it a little, and shows
it, saying:*

The body of Christ.

The communicant answers:

Amen.(5)

and receives communion.

*When a deacon gives communion, he does
the same.*

*The sign of communion is more complete
when given under both kinds, since the sign
of the eucharistic meal appears more clearly.
The intention of Christ that the new and
eternal covenant be ratified in his blood is
better expressed, as is the relation of the
eucharistic banquet to the heavenly banquet.*

*When he presents the chalice, the priest or
deacon says:*

The blood of Christ.(6)

The communicant answers:

Amen.

and drinks it.

COMMUNION SONG

*While the priest receives the body of Christ,
the communion song is begun.*

*The vessels are cleansed by the priest or
deacon or acolyte after the communion or
after Mass, if possible at the side table.*

Meanwhile he says inaudibly:

(4) In what ways has God healed you?

(5) What is your experience of Communion like?
When the experience is really outstanding, what
has made it that way for you?

(6) In what ways is receiving from the cup
different from receiving the consecrated bread?

Reflection 1: Breaking of the Bread through Prayer after Communion (page 3)

Lord, may I receive these gifts in purity of
    heart.
May they bring me healing and strength, now
    and for ever.

PERIOD OF SILENCE OR SONG OF PRAISE(7)

*Then the priest may return to the chair. A
period of silence may now be observed, or a
psalm or song of praise may be sung.*

PRAYER AFTER COMMUNION

*Then, standing at the chair or at the altar, the
priest sings or says:*

Let us pray.

*Priest and people pray in silence for a while,
unless a period of silence has already been
observed. Then the priest extends his hands
and sings or says the prayer after
communion...*

Almighty God,
we receive new life
from the supper your Son gave us in this
    world.
May we find full contentment
in the meal we hope to share
in your eternal kingdom.
We ask this through Christ our Lord.

...at the end of which the people respond:

Amen.

(7) What do you do with the silence after Communion? How does the song of praise affect you?

Intent 1:
Breaking of the Bread *through* Prayer after Communion

BREAKING OF THE BREAD(1)

Then the following is sung or said:

Lamb of God, you take away the sins of the
    world:
  have mercy on us.
Lamb of God, you take away the sins of the
    world:
  have mercy on us.
Lamb of God, you take away the sins of the
    world:
  grant us peace.

*[The "Lamb of God"] may be repeated until
the breaking of the bread is finished, but the
last phrase is always "Grant us peace."*

*Meanwhile, he takes the host and breaks it
over the paten. He places a small piece in the
chalice, saying inaudibly:*

May this mingling of the body and blood of
  our Lord Jesus Christ
bring eternal life to us who receive it.

PRIVATE PREPARATION OF THE PRIEST

*Then the priest joins his hands and says
inaudibly:*

Lord Jesus Christ, Son of the living God, by
the will of the Father and the work of the Holy
Spirit your death brought life to the world. By
your holy body and blood free me from all my
sins, and from every evil. Keep me faithful to
your teaching, and never let me be parted
from you.

COMMUNION(2)

*The priest genuflects. Taking the host, he
raises it slightly over the paten and, facing the
people, says aloud:*

This is the Lamb of God
who takes away the sins of the world.
Happy are those who are called to his supper.

He adds, once only, with the people:

(1) The Breaking of the Bread is an important
action in the Communion Rite. It is also called
the Fraction Rite. It is a powerful symbol of the
assembly's oneness: "in sharing in the one
bread of life which is Christ we who are many
are made one body" (GI 56c). The Breaking of
the Bread was so important to early Christians
that they called what is our "Mass" the "breaking of the bread." It is a sign not only of unity
but also of charity "since the one bread is being
distributed among the members of one family"
(GI 283).

The Breaking of the Bread has a strong biblical
basis: "Because the loaf of bread is one, we,
though many, are one body, for we all partake
of the one loaf" (1 Cor 10:17).

Once individual, ready-made wafers began to be
used (in the tenth century), this once powerful
and moving symbol of unity was lost.

(2) Communion under both species (bread and
wine, now body and blood) "has a more complete form as a sign when it is received under
both kinds....[T]here is a clearer expression of
that will by which the new and everlasting
covenant is ratified in the blood of the Lord and
of the relationship of the eucharistic banquet to
the eschatological banquet in the Father's kingdom" (GI 240).

Intent 1: Breaking of the Bread through Prayer after Communion (page 2)

Lord, I am not worthy to receive you,
but only say the word and I shall be healed.

Facing the altar, the priest says inaudibly:

May the body of Christ bring me to
everlasting life.

*He reverently consumes the body of Christ.
Then he takes the chalice and says inaudibly:*

May the blood of Christ bring me to
    everlasting life.

He reverently drinks the blood of Christ.

*After this he takes the paten or other vessel
and goes to the communicants. He takes a
host for each one, raises it a little, and shows
it, saying:*

The body of Christ.(3)

The communicant answers:

Amen.(4)

and receives communion.

*When a deacon gives communion, he does
the same.*

*The sign of communion is more complete
when given under both kinds, since the sign
of the eucharistic meal appears more clearly.
The intention of Christ that the new and
eternal covenant be ratified in his blood is
better expressed, as is the relation of the
eucharistic banquet to the heavenly banquet.*

*When he presents the chalice, the priest or
deacon says:*

The blood of Christ.

The communicant answers:

Amen.(4)

and drinks it.

COMMUNION SONG(5)

*While the priest receives the body of Christ,
the communion song is begun.*

*The vessels are cleansed by the priest or
deacon or acolyte after the communion or
after Mass, if possible at the side table.*

Meanwhile he says inaudibly:

(3) Communion received in the hand is the older form of reception. Communion on the tongue became the accepted practice during the ninth century as a symbol of exaggerated unworthiness. In 1977, we returned to Communion in the hand as a more natural response to the words of Jesus, "Take and eat." Communion distribution should be done reverently and unhurriedly to allow the reception of Communion to reach fulfillment as an expression of complete and total faith.

(4) This "Amen" is a "Yes" to three different things: "yes" to the presence of Christ in the assembly, "yes" to the presence of Christ in the communicant, and "yes" to the presence of Christ in the bread and the wine. "As we receive the bread in our hands and pronounce our Amen, we give voice to our acceptance of ourselves as we are in Christ" (Manly and Reinhard 304).

(5) The Communion Song expresses "outwardly the communicants' union in spirit by means of the unity of their voices, to give evidence of joy of heart, and to make the procession to receive Christ's body more fully an act of community" (GI 56i).

Intent 1: Breaking of the Bread through Prayer after Communion (page 3)

Lord, may I receive these gifts in purity of
  heart.
May they bring me healing and strength,
  now and for ever.

PERIOD OF SILENCE OR SONG OF PRAISE(6)

*Then the priest may return to the chair. A
period of silence may now be observed, or a
psalm or song of praise may be sung.*

PRAYER AFTER COMMUNION(7)

*Then, standing at the chair or at the altar, the
priest sings or says:*

Let us pray.

*Priest and people pray in silence for a while,
unless a period of silence has already been
observed. Then the priest extends his hands
and sings or says the prayer after
communion...*

Almighty God,
we receive new life
from the supper your Son gave us in this
  world.
May we find full contentment
in the meal we hope to share
in your eternal kingdom.
We ask this through Christ our Lord.

...at the end of which the people respond:

Amen.

(6) The silence after the vessels are cleansed can
be a time for meditation, a reflection on the
transforming power of Christ. A hymn may also
be sung at this time, one of praise and thanks
for our invitation to and participation in this
most marvelous of all banquets, the eucharistic
banquet.

(7) The Prayer after Communion has a specific
focus; it is a prayer of petition that the Eucharist
that we have just eaten, the meal we have just
celebrated, will produce in us the effects of the
mystery as Jesus envisioned and instructed in
the Gospels. This particular prayer is taken from
Holy Thursday, Mass of the Lord's Supper.

Reflection 2: Concluding Rite

CONCLUDING RITE

If there are any brief announcements, they are made at this time.

GREETING

The rite of dismissal takes place.

Facing the people, the priest extends his hands and sings or says:

The Lord be with you.

The people answer:

And also with you.

BLESSING

Deacon:

Bow your heads and pray for God's blessing.

The Father of mercies has given us an
   example of unselfish love(1)
in the sufferings of his only Son.
Through your service of God and neighbor
may you receive his countless blessings(2).

R. Amen.

You believe that by his dying
Christ destroyed death forever(3).
May he give you everlasting life.

R. Amen.

He humbled himself for our sakes.
May you follow his example(4)
and share in his resurrection.

R. Amen.

The priest always concludes the solemn blessing by adding:

May almighty God bless you(5),
the Father, and the Son, ✠ and the Holy Spirit.

The people answer:

Amen.

(1) How does this unselfish love make you feel?

(2) Do you experience the service of God and neighbor as a blessing for yourself? What is that like?

(3) How is your belief in this statement strengthened? What does it mean for you personally?

(4) How does your experience of liturgy help you follow Jesus' example?

(5) How do you experience this blessing? What helps you to be more aware of it?

Reflection 2: Concluding Rite (page 2)

(6) What is your personal response to this?

DISMISSAL

The dismissal sends each member of the congregation to do good works, praising and blessing the Lord.

The deacon (or the priest), with hands joined, sings or says:

Go in peace to love and serve the Lord(6).

The people answer:

Thanks be to God.

The priest kisses the altar as at the beginning. Then he makes the customary reverence with the ministers and leaves.

Intent 2: Concluding Rite

Liturgy is both celebration and preparation. It prepares us to go forth to love and serve. Therefore, the Concluding Rite is far from a "conclusion" as in the ending of a good book or the school year. It is more of a commissioning that takes as its basis the commissioning Jesus gave to his apostles in the post-resurrection Gospel stories: "Go, therefore, and make disciples of all nations" (Mt 28:19); "Go into the whole world and proclaim the gospel to every creature" (Mk 16:15); "repentance, for the forgiveness of sins, would be preached in his name to all the nations, beginning from Jerusalem" (Lk 24:47); "As the Father has sent me, so I send you" (Jn 20:21). Strengthened by our celebration, we are to evangelize, proclaim the Gospel, preach acts of forgiveness, and be sent as Jesus was sent.

Johannes Emminghaus makes an interesting observation regarding the shortness of the rite: "The reason why it was never properly developed may be that frequent Communion ceased rather early in the Church's history and the faithful left the church in large numbers before the Communion of the priest" (208).

The rite consists of a Greeting, Blessing, and Dismissal, which sends the people forth.

Any brief announcements should be made prior to the greeting. This is also the place to read letters from the bishop, etc.

(1) The Greeting is in the same format as the Greeting (form C) used in the Introductory Rites and the dialogue that begins the Eucharistic Prayer. The exchange serves to draw us together one last time before we are sent forth to love and serve.

CONCLUDING RITE

If there are any brief announcements, they are made at this time.

GREETING(1)

The rite of dismissal takes place.

Facing the people, the priest extends his hands and sings or says:

The Lord be with you.

The people answer:

And also with you.

Eucharist!

Intent 2: Concluding Rite (page 2)

BLESSING(2)

Deacon:

Bow your heads and pray for God's blessing.

The Father of mercies has given us an
  example of unselfish love
in the sufferings of his only Son.
Through your service of God and neighbor
may you receive his countless blessings.

R. Amen.

You believe that by his dying
Christ destroyed death forever.
May he give you everlasting life.

R. Amen.

He humbled himself for our sakes.
May you follow his example
and share in his resurrection.

R. Amen.

*The priest always concludes the solemn
blessing by adding:*

May almighty God bless you,
the Father, and the Son, ✠ and the Holy
  Spirit.(3)

The people answer:

Amen.

DISMISSAL(4)

*The dismissal sends each member of the
congregation to do good works, praising and
blessing the Lord.*

*The deacon (or the priest), with hands joined,
sings or says:*

Go in peace to love and serve the Lord.

The people answer:

Thanks be to God.

*The priest kisses the altar as at the beginning.
Then he makes the customary reverence with
the ministers and leaves.*

(2) There are three options for the Blessing. The
first is a simple blessing. The second is a solemn
blessing, such as the one used here, which is
the fifth solemn blessing, the one used for the
Passion of the Lord. There are twenty solemn
blessings in all: some for particular seasons
(Advent, Christmas, etc.), five for Ordinary
Time, four for celebrations of saints, and two in
the "other" category (for dedication of a church
and for the dead). The third option is a prayer
over the people. The Sacramentary offers
twenty-six different texts for these prayers.
When the solemn blessing or the prayer over the
people is used, the deacon or priest invites the
people to bow their heads to pray for God's
blessing; this is not done with the simple blessing. With either the solemn blessing or the
prayer over the people, the priest always
extends both hands over the people as a visual
sign of bestowing the blessing.

(3) With every form of blessing, the priest calls
upon the Trinity, which complements the trinitarian greeting of the Introductory Rites. Thus
we see there is rhythm and planning to the
entire liturgy.

(4) The word "dismissal" and the word "Mass"
are forms of the same Latin word, *mittere*, which
means "to send." The words "Go in peace" are
the words Jesus used when he dismissed the
woman he had cured of the hemorrhage (Mk
5:34).

Liturgy and Agape Checklist

Whole Group:

- ☐ Select Scriptures. You may use the Scriptures for the day or ones that are appropriate for your community.

- ☐ Based on the Scriptures, pick appropriate music. Make sure that you work closely with the cantor when choosing the following sung parts of the Mass:

  - ◊ Acclamations: "Alleluia"; "Holy, Holy, Holy"; Memorial Acclamation; Great Amen; Doxology to the Lord's Prayer

  - ◊ Processional songs for the Entrance and Communion

  - ◊ Responsorial Psalm

- ☐ Decide if you will sing other parts of the Mass and which setting you will use.

  - ◊ Gloria

  - ◊ Lord's Prayer

  - ◊ "Lamb of God"

- ☐ Decide if you will have supplementary songs and what they will be.

  - ◊ Altar Preparation

  - ◊ Recessional

- ☐ Pick volunteers for the following:

  - ◊ First Reading

  - ◊ Second Reading

  - ◊ General Intercessions

  - ◊ Presentation of Gifts

  - ◊ flowers for altar

  - ◊ baker of eucharistic bread

Group One: General Intercessions

- ☐ Write the General Intercessions, making sure you have one for each of the four groups:

  - ◊ Church

  - ◊ world

  - ◊ those in need

  - ◊ local community

Group Two: Liturgical Text

- ☐ Do you want a Rite of Blessing and Sprinkling Holy Water (which replace the Penitential Rite and the Kyrie)?

- ☐ Choose the liturgical texts for the following:

  - ◊ Penitential Rite (form A, B or C)

  - ◊ Eucharistic Prayer (we recommend one of the two for the Masses of Reconciliation)

  - ◊ If you use Eucharistic Prayer I or III, select the Preface that you want (II and IV have their own).

- ☐ Decide which, if any, solemn blessing or prayer over the people you will use.

Group Three: Agape Meal

- ☐ Assess your facility, including appliances, dishes and tableware. In terms of preparation, what is possible? In terms of serving and eating, what will you need?

- ☐ Determine your basic menu and who will bring what, remembering to include those in the other groups.

- ☐ Determine what incidentals you will need, including drinks, paper goods, condiments, etc.

Liturgy Preparation Sheet

Note: During the liturgy, make sure there is time during the General Intercessions for people to add their own intentions out loud and in silence. Also, make sure that you ask the priest to allow time during the Sign of Peace for the Sending of Peace to all those who are not present.

Entrance Song: _____

Penitential Rite: _____

Gloria
    ☐ Recited
    ☐ Sung/Setting:_____

First Reading/Reader: _____
_____

Responsorial Psalm: _____

Second Reading/Reader:_____
_____

Alleluia Setting:_____

Gospel: _____

General Intercessions Reader: _____

Presentation of Gifts (2 people):
_____
_____

Song for Preparation of Altar and Gifts:
_____

Eucharistic Prayer: _____

Preface (if using Eucharistic Prayer I or III):
_____

"Holy, Holy, Holy" Setting: _____

Memorial Acclamation:_____

Great Amen Setting: _____

Lord's Prayer
    ☐ Recited
    ☐ Sung/Setting:_____

"Lamb of God"
    ☐ Recited
    ☐ Sung/Setting:_____

Communion Song:_____

Solemn Blessing or Prayer over the People:
_____

Recessional Song: _____

Flowers:_____

Bread Baker: _____

Program Evaluation

1. Did this program meet your goals? Please say a few general things about your experience.

_____

_____

_____

2. Did the prayer experiences make the part of the liturgy to which they pertained more meaningful? Which was the most significant for you?

_____

_____

_____

3. In what ways were the reflection questions useful? If you did not find them helpful, what would have made them so?

_____

_____

_____

4. What was the group sharing portion of the program like for you?

_____

_____

_____

5. Was the intent part of our program (having the words, actions and symbols and some of the background/history of the liturgy explained) useful? In what way?

_____

_____

_____

Eucharist!

Program Evaluation (page 2)

6. What is the primary benefit you have received from this program?

_____

_____

_____

7. What would you like to have seen more of? What would you like to have seen less of?

_____

_____

_____

8. What was the most moving part of the program for you and why?

_____

_____

_____

9. In what ways could your presenter(s) have been more helpful and/or responsive to your needs and questions?

_____

_____

_____

Please write any additional comments below:

Session 8:
Celebration of Eucharist and Agape

We celebrate God's presence in our lives,
and we are drawn "into the compelling love of Christ and set on fire."

Schedule

Time	Description
5 minutes	Gathering Prayer
20 minutes	Reflection: Sharing Experiences of the Program
75 minutes	Celebration of Eucharist
10 minutes	Prayer 1: Signing of the Senses
5 minutes	Prayer 2: Namasté
45 minutes	Agape Meal

Resource Sheets

Overview

This session concludes your program. While the celebration of Eucharist is of primary importance, this session is also an opportunity to honor the bonds that you have developed and nurtured over the course of the time you have been together and also an opportunity for good-byes. Those of us in the fields of spiritual direction or counseling might use the more imposing words, "termination" or "closure."

Preceding the celebration of Eucharist, there is a short reflection period. The Eucharist "concludes" with a Signing of the Senses, which is adapted from one of the rites of initiation from the Rite of Christian Initiation of Adults. If you wish, you may conclude the program by honoring of God's presence in the program, in all of creation and in each other through a prayer we call Namasté, which we have adapted from the Hindu tradition.

Depending on the type of meal that you have chosen, the reflection, Eucharist and signing may either precede or follow it. If you have chosen to gather in the evening and have a full meal, the meal may, for practicality's sake, precede the rest of the session. If you have chosen to gather in the evening and have coffee and dessert, it might be convenient to have the meal follow the rest of the session. If you have chosen to gather in the morning, you might choose to have a brunch that follows the session. We have done both a coffee and dessert type of meal and a brunch and they work equally well.

The schedule for this session is a bit tight. You may want to extend your session by half an hour. As the schedule stands now, you have two hours and forty minutes of filled time, and this only allows for a forty-five-minute meal. You may need more time than that, depending on what type of meal you have planned. You may also need more than one hour and fifteen minutes for Eucharist.

Gathering Prayer

See Session 2, page 54, for Gathering Prayer.

Reflection: Sharing Experiences of the Program

Invite the participants of the program to share their thoughts or feelings around the experience of the program. You may use the Presenter's Reflection Questions on this page or the questions from

Presenter's Reflection Questions

As you prepare for Session 8, you might ponder or bring to prayer the following questions:

◊ Reflecting on your own experience of the program, what has touched you the most? Surprised you? Challenged you?

◊ What are your feelings around ending the program? What is your sense of the group as they contemplate completion of the program?

◊ When have you most been able to express your feelings around "closure" or "termination" or simply around completing a process or long-term project?

◊ How might you help the participants in the program do the same?

Just as the bread broken was first scattered on the hills, then was gathered and became one, so let your Church be gathered from the ends of the earth into our kingdom, for yours is glory and power through all ages! Amen.
—Didache,
in Emminghaus 27

the Program Evaluation in Session 7. Participants may want to share with the group the symbol they have brought to place at the foot of the altar.

Celebration of Eucharist

Process to the church for your celebration of Eucharist.

Prayer 1: Signing of the Senses

Introduction

This prayer is an adaptation of the Signing of the Senses, one of the rituals used during the Rite of Christian Initiation of Adults. It lends itself well to the final invitation of the liturgy to "Go in peace to love and serve the Lord." It is an experience of serving each other that, in conjunction with the Namasté prayer, offers a sense of closure to the program.

Outline

1. Ask the group to line up in pairs; if there is an odd number, create one triad.

2. Participants face each other and trace the sign of the cross lightly upon or over the part of the body to which you refer in each section of the prayer.

3. Each person completes the tracing on their partner before the other begins. The tracing needs to be done slowly and with reverence, mindfulness and prayerfulness.

4. The final sign of the cross extends from the top of the head to the feet and from shoulder to shoulder. Explain this before you begin prayer so as not to interrupt the rhythm of the action during the prayer. Some people may have physical limitations that make signing the feet or the entire being difficult; encourage them to do as best they can. If they cannot reach their partners' feet, explain that the intention is what is important.

Presenter Preparation

Your own preparation for prayer should include the following:

◊ Photocopy the text of the prayer, pages 186-187, for yourself.

Details

Remind the group that, even though you are the only one praying aloud, they are to pray the words in their hearts as they trace the sign of the cross.

Pace the prayer, praying slowly, continuing to be aware of the entire group. When everyone is done with the signing of one part, move on to the next, but do not rush.

Prayer 2: Namasté

Introduction

This prayer immediately follows the Signing of the Senses. It is based upon the ritual of Namasté. It is a Hindu practice, which involves the action of bringing the palms of the hands together, fingers extended, in a gesture of prayer. The hands are raised until the index fingers touch the forehead and then the person bows deeply. The action is accompanied by a deeply embodied experience of "I recognize, greet and honor the divine presence within you."

We recommend this prayer as a way of ritually giving thanks for the experience of the program and for the gift each person has been to the program and to each other. We hope that this expression of thanksgiving will be a gentle way of bringing your program to a close.

The prayer is done in silence except for the brief introductory prayer that accompanies each experience of bowing.

Outline

1. Ask the group to form one complete circle.
2. Invite everyone to bow to the center of the circle.
3. Invite everyone to turn around so that they face away from the center of the circle. They bow again.
4. Invite everyone to turn to the inside of the circle one last time; they bow to each other. The bowing in this instance is done by making eye contact with each person and then bowing to each other at the same time. This may take a while, depending on the size of your group. It can be a powerful experience.

Presenter Preparation

Your own preparation for prayer should include the following:

◊ Make one photocopy of the text of the prayer, page 188, for yourself.

Lord,
as you give us the body
  and blood of your Son,
guide us with your Spirit
that we may honor you
not only with our lips,
but also with the lives we
  lead,
and so enter your
  kingdom.
          —Prayer after
            Communion,
            Ninth Sunday
            in Ordinary Time

Lord,
we pray for your people
  who believe in you.
May they enjoy the gift
  of your love,
share it with others,
and spread it
  everywhere.
          —Prayer over
            the People 9

Details

Bowing is a motion that involves mind, body and spirit. When you bow, you bow with total awareness of the divine presence in that toward which you bow. Every molecule of your being should be filled, speaking the words, "I recognize, greet and honor the divine presence within you." The bow should be done with complete mindfulness and prayerfulness. You may want to invite participants to practice bowing before actually beginning the prayer.

Agape Meal

This concludes Session 8.

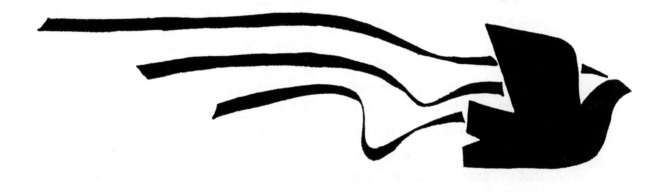

Session 8 Resource Sheets

Prayer 1: Signing of the Senses

Opening Prayer

The presider begins with the following or similar words:

> Tender Father and Mother of all mercy and love,
> we thank you for your call to us to serve you and one another.
> You have sought and summoned us in many ways
> and we have turned to seek you.
> You have called us and we have answered by our presence.
> We praise you, Gentle God, and we bless you.

The presider invites each person to gently trace the sign of the cross on or over each part of the body, continuing to pray:

> As we make the sign of the cross on our foreheads, we pray:
>
> Receive the sign of the cross on your forehead,
> that you may continue to grow in your knowledge of the God who loves you.
> (*Pause.*)
>
> As we make the sign of the cross on our ears, we pray:
>
> Receive the sign of the cross on your ears,
> that you may hear more clearly the voice of the Lord. (*Pause.*)
>
> As we make the sign of the cross on our eyes, we pray:
>
> Receive the sign of the cross on your eyes,
> that you may see more completely the face of God in others and in the world.
> (*Pause.*)
>
> As we make the sign of the cross on our lips, we pray:
>
> Receive the sign of the cross on your lips,
> that you may speak more openly of God's love to others. (*Pause.*)
>
> As we make the sign of the cross on our hearts, we pray:
>
> Receive the sign of the cross over your heart,
> for that is where Christ dwells within you. (*Pause.*)
>
> As we make the sign of the cross on our shoulders, we pray:
>
> Receive the sign of the cross on your shoulders,
> that you may bear more willingly the yoke of Christ. (*Pause.*)
>
> As we make the sign of the cross on our hands, we pray:
>
> Receive the sign of the cross on your hands,
> that your work may always be Christ's work. (*Pause.*)

Prayer 1: Signing of the Senses (page 2)

As we make the sign of the cross on our feet, we pray:

Receive the sign of the cross on your feet,
that you may walk more confidently in the footsteps of Christ. (*Pause.*)

As we make the sign of the cross on our entire being, we pray:

Receive the sign of the cross into your entire being,
that you may bear more passionately the presence of Christ to the world. (*Pause.*)

Closing Prayer

Presider concludes the signing with the following prayer or similar words:

Generous God, source of all creation,
you have lovingly made us in your image and likeness.
With a deepened sense of commitment,
send us forth with tender hearts and open hands.
We have listened to the call of Christ.
Through the power of his call, renew us.
With your grace, refashion us, that we may become the full likeness of Christ.
Amen.

Prayer 2: Namasté

Bowing to the Center of the Circle

As all bow to the center of the circle, presider prays in these or similar words:

> We bow to the divine presence within our group,
> the God who has been among us, who has guided us, informed us,
> cradled us and called us to be a royal priesthood, a chosen people,
> a people loved and treasured and created in God's image.

Bowing to the Outside of the Circle

As all turn and bow to the outside of the circle, presider prays in these or similar words:

> We bow to the divine presence, the God who is in all creation,
> who has spoken through all living things.
> We bow to all the directions of the earth: north, south, east and west.
> We bow to all the seasons of the year: winter, spring, summer, and fall.
> As part of a circle that is so intimately connected, when one bows, we all bow.
> Hearts overflowing, our gratitude pours out upon all that is.

Bowing to One Another

As all turn to one another, presider prays in these or similar words:

> We bow to the divine presence who dwells within each one of us,
> the God who has spoken through our words and actions.
> We bow with heartfelt thanksgiving for the gift we have all been to one another
> as we have journeyed these many weeks together,
> as we have prayed and laughed and wept together—
> as we have been Christ to one another.

Works Cited and Recommended

Books and Periodicals

Baldovin, John, S.J. *Worship: City, Church and Renewal.* Washington, DC: Pastoral Press, 1991.

Bergan, Jacqueline Syrup, and S. Marie Schwan. *Freedom: A Guide for Prayer.* Winona, Minnesota: St. Mary's Press, 1988.

Ciferni, Andrew D., O.Praem. "This Saving Cup." Washington, DC: Federation of Diocesan Liturgical Commissions, 1991.

Ciferni, Andrew D., OFM, and Elizabeth Hoffman. "The Eucharistic Prayer—Center and Summit?" *Liturgy 90* 23, no. 4 (May/June 1992): 4-6, 15.

Collins, Mary, OSB. *Worship: Renewal to Practice.* Washington, DC: Pastoral Press, 1987.

Conn, Walter. *Christian Conversion: A Developmental Interpretation of Autonomy and Surrender.* Mahwah, New Jersey: Paulist Press, 1986.

Cooke, Bernard. "Sacraments." In *The New Dictionary of Sacramental Worship,* edited by Peter Fink, SJ, 1116-1123. Collegeville, Minnesota: Liturgical Press, 1991.

Duffy, Regis A. *Real Presence: Worship, Sacraments and Commitment.* New York: Harper & Row, 1982.

Earth Prayers from around the World: 365 Prayers, Poems, and Invocations for Honoring the Earth. Edited by Elizabeth Roberts and Elias Amidon. New York: HarperCollins, 1991.

Emminghaus, Johannes H. *Eucharist: Essence, Form, Celebration.* Collegeville, Minnesota: Liturgical Press, 1976.

Empereur, James. *Worship: Exploring the Sacred.* Washington, DC: Pastoral Press, 1987.

Fink, Peter. *Worship: Praying the Sacraments.* Washington, DC: Pastoral Press, 1991.

Fischer, Balthasar. *Signs, Words and Gestures..* New York: Pueblo Press, 1981.

Gallen, John, SJ. "Assembly." In *The New Dictionary of Sacramental Worship,* edited by Peter Fink, SJ, 71-80. Collegeville, Minnesota: Liturgical Press, 1991.

Gentry-Akin, David. "To Make Eucharist Is To Give Thanks." *Creation* 5, no. 1 (January-February 1989): 42-43.

Guzie, Tad. "Reclaiming the Eucharist." *Liturgy* 7, no. 1 (Summer 1987): 29-33.

Irwin, Kevin. *Liturgy, Prayer and Spirituality.* New York: Paulist Press, 1984.

Johnson, Lawrence J. *The Word and Eucharist Handbook.* Rev. ed. San Jose, California: Resource Publications, Inc., 1993.

Jorgensen, Susan S. *Rekindling the Passion: Liturgical Renewal in Your Community.* San Jose, California: Resource Publications, Inc., 1993.

————. "The Dismissal Rite: A Blessing for Action." *Modern Liturgy* 19, no. 8 (October 1992): 18-21.

Kolodziej, Maynard, OFM. "Typology of the Exodus—Passover." In *Understanding the Mass.* Pulaski, Wisconsin: Franciscan Publishers, 1987.

Krosnicki, Thomas A. "Preparing the Gifts: Clarifying the Rite." *Worship* 65, no. 2 (March 1991): 149-159.

Lathrop, Gordon. "Chronicle: AIDS and the Cup." *Worship* 62, no. 2 (March 1988): 161-165.

————. "How Symbols Speak." *Liturgy* 7, no. 1 (Summer 1987): 9-13.

The Liturgy Documents: A Parish Resource. 3rd ed. Edited by Elizabeth Hoffman. Chicago, Illinois: Liturgy Training Publications, 1991.

Manly, Gregory, and Anneliese Reinhard. *The Art of Praying Liturgy.* Melbourne: Spectrum Publications, 1984.

Marcheschi, Graziano. "Don't Be a Pew Potato (Or, How to Hear the Word of God)." *Praying* 38 (September/October 1990): 5-6.

McManus, Frederick. *Liturgical Participation: An Ongoing Assessment.* Washington, DC: Pastoral Press, 1988.

Moore, Thomas. *Care of the Soul: A Guide for Cultivating Depth and Sacredness in Everyday Life.* New York: Harper Collins, 1992.

Nocent, Adrian. *The Liturgical Year: Advent,Christmas, Epiphany.* Collegeville, Minnesota: The Liturgical Press, 1977.

————. *The Liturgical Year: Lent and Holy Week.* Collegeville, Minnesota: The Liturgical Press, 1977.

————. *The Liturgical Year: Sundays in Ordinary Time.* Collegeville, Minnesota: The Liturgical Press, 1977.

————. *The Liturgical Year: The Easter Season.* Collegeville, Minnesota: The Liturgical Press, 1977.

Ostdiek, Gilbert. *Catechesis for Liturgy.* Washington, DC: Pastoral Press, 1986.

————. "Liturgical Catechesis." In *The New Dictionary of Sacramental Worship,* edited by Peter Fink, SJ, 163-172. Collegeville, Minnesota: The Liturgical Press, 1991.

Peace Prayers: Meditations, Affirmations, Invocations, Poems, and Prayers for Peace. Edited by the staff of HarperSan Francisco. New York: HarperCollins, 1992.

Piercy, Robert. "Making Bread for Eucharist." *Liturgy 90* 23, no. 2 (February/March 1992): 4-5.

Pleiness, Gregg A. "You and I are Eucharist." *Living Prayer* 21, no. 3 (May-June 1988): 18-21.

Powers, Joseph M., SJ. "Ministry." In *The New Dictionary of Sacramental Worship*, edited by Peter Fink, SJ, 828-837. Collegeville, Minnesota: The Liturgical Press, 1991.

Ryan, G. Thomas. "The Sacramentary: Sourcebook for Pastoral Ministry." *Liturgy 90* 23, no. 8 (November-December 1992): 4-7.

Ryan, John Barry. "Eucharistic Prayers." In *The New Dictionary of Sacramental Worship*, edited by Peter Fink, SJ, 451-458. Collegeville, Minnesota: The Liturgical Press, 1991.

Saliers, Don E. "Sanctifying Time, Place and People: Rhythms of Worship and Spirituality." *Weavings* 2, no. 5 (September-October 1987): 18-28.

Searle, Mark. "On the Art of Lifting up the Heart: Liturgical Prayer Today." *Studies in Formative Spirituality* 3 (November 1982): 399-410.

Skublics, Ernest. "Psychologically Living Symbolism and Liturgy." In *Carl Jung and Christian Spirituality*, edited by Robert L. Moore, 206-227. Mahwah, New Jersey: Paulist Press, 1988.

Smalley, Gary, and John Trent, PhD. *The Blessing*. Nashville: Thomas Nelson Publishers, 1986.

Stauffer, S. Anita. "The Why of Worship." *Worship* 65, no. 1 (January 1989): 45-49.

Steere, Douglas V. "Intercession: Caring for Souls." *Weavings* 4, no. 2 (March-April 1989): 17-26.

Steindl-Rast, David. *Gratefulness, The Heart of Prayer*. New York: Paulist Press, 1984.

Teilhard de Chardin, Pierre. "Mass on the World." *Hymn of the Universe*. New York: Harper & Row, 1961.

Thurian, Max. *The Mystery of the Eucharist*. Grand Rapids, Michigan: William B. Erdman's Publishing Co., 1984.

Valiquette, Hilaire, OFM. "What the Our Father Really Says." *St. Anthony Messenger* 92 (November 1976): 38-41.

Webster's New Twentieth Century Dictionary of the English Language (Unabridged). 2nd ed. Edited by Jean L. McKechnie. N.p.: Collins World, 1977.

Woolfenden, Graham. "'Let us offer each other the sign of peace'—An Enquiry." *Worship* 67, no. 3 (May 1993): 239-252.

Zimmerman, Joyce A. "The General Intercessions: Yet Another Visit." *Worship* 65, no. 4 (July 1991): 306-319.

Music

Berkey, Jackson. *Fresh Aire Interludes*. Omaha: American Gramaphone Records, 1981.

Foley, John. "Take, Lord, Receive." Phoenix: North American Liturgy Resources, 1975.

———. "One Bread, One Body." Portland, Oregon: New Dawn Music, 1976.

Haas, David. "Song of the Body of Christ." *Creating God*. Chicago: GIA Publications, 1989.

Hardman, James. *The River*. Eastsound, Orca Island, Washington: Anahata, 1990.

Jones, Michael. *After the Rain*. Milwaukee: Narada Publications, 1988.

Landry, Carey. "Peace Is Flowing Like a River." Phoenix: North American Liturgy Resources, 1975.

Lanz, David. *Heartsounds*. Milwaukee: Narada Publications, 1983.

Sun, David. *Peace*. Edina, Minnesota: Sun Productions. 1984.

Talbot, John Michael. "Heart of the Shepherd." Sparrow Corporation, Birdwing Music, 1987.

Temple, Sebastian. "Prayer of St. Francis." Franciscan Communications Center, 1967.

Winter, Miriam Therese. "Sing of a Blessing." Philadelphia: Medical Mission Sisters, 1987.

Liturgy Resources

From the author of *Eucharist!*

REKINDLING THE PASSION:
Liturgical Renewal in Your Community
Susan S. Jorgensen
Paper, 272 pages, 5½" x 8½", $14.95
ISBN 0-89390-236-5

This book provides the theory behind the eight-session ritual-catechesis experience of *Eucharist!* Jorgensen examines Vatican II's vision, liturgy as ritual, the people as the Body of Christ, symbolism, personal and cultural maturity, and pastoral care—all as they relate to liturgical renewal. Spiritual directors, liturgists, pastors, religious educators—anyone trying to connect personal and communal prayer—will want this book in their libraries.

THE WORD AND EUCHARIST HANDBOOK
Lawrence J. Johnson
Paper, 268 pages, 6" X 9", $11.95, ISBN 0-89390-276-4

A complete reference guide for worship planners, ministers, and liturgical artists, this book answers your questions about the origin, development, and modern practice of each part of the Mass. Revised edition includes updated bibliography.

EVALUATING YOUR LITURGICAL MUSIC MINISTRY
Keith L. Patterson
Paper, 160 pages, 8½" X 11", $19.95, ISBN 0-89390-258-6

This book includes all the information you need for surveying and measuring the quality and effectiveness of your present liturgical music, then guides you in implementing liturgically correct changes to improve your community's worship experience.

Small Group Resources

ACTS OF APOSTLES:
Building Faith Communities
Paper, 200 pages, 5½" x 8½", $14.95, ISBN 0-89390-292-6

LEADER'S GUIDE TO *ACTS OF APOSTLES*
Paper, 48 pages, 5½" x 8½", $6.95, ISBN 0-89390-300-0
both by Leonard Doohan, PhD

Dr. Doohan's commentary will inspire you to adapt Luke's vision of church as a model for building your own faith community. The *Leader's Guide*, designed for study group leaders and religious studies educators, will help you share the message of Acts with your community.

MOMS: DEVELOPING A MINISTRY
Paula Hagen & Patricia Hoyt
Paper, 160 pages, 8½" x 11", $19.95, ISBN 0-89390-228-4

This comprehensive manual is filled with resources and guidelines for setting up a Ministry of Mothers Sharing (MOMS) program in your community. Includes lesson plans, job descriptions for leaders, administrative and publicity procedures, and reproducible handouts. See next column for accompanying resources.

MOMS FACILITATOR'S GUIDE
Paula Hagen, Vickie LoPiccolo Jennett,
& Patricia Hoyt
Paper, 144 pages, 8½" x 11", $11.95, ISBN 0-89390-256-X

Includes everything both the first-time and seasoned facilitator need to lead a MOMS support group.

MOMS: A PERSONAL JOURNAL
Paula Hagen with Vickie LoPiccolo Jennett
Paper, 112 pages, 7" X 10", $9.95, ISBN 0-89390-224-1

A series of reflections that allows mothers of school-age children to look at their values, the choices they make each day, and the love they share with others.

A PRAYER COMPANION FOR MOMS
Vickie LoPiccolo Jennett with Paula Hagen
Paper, 104 pages, 4" X 6", $6.95, ISBN 0-89390-265-9

Any mother will enjoy these reflections on such daily experiences as juggling schedules, cleaning the refrigerator, waiting in line, and taking time out for fun. Includes space to write your own thoughts and feelings as well.

Order Form

Order these resources from your local bookstore, or mail this form to:

QTY	TITLE	PRICE	TOTAL

Subtotal: _____

CA residents add 7¼% sales tax
(Santa Clara Co. residents, 8¼%): _____

Postage and handling
($2 for order up to $20; 10% of order over $20 but less than $150; $15 for order of $150 or more): _____

Total: _____

Resource Publications, Inc.
160 E. Virginia Street #290 - TX
San Jose, CA 95112-5876
(408) 286-8505 or FAX (408) 287-8748

☐ My check or money order is enclosed.
☐ Charge my ☐ VISA ☐ MC. Expiration Date_____

Card #_____-_____-_____-_____
Signature _____
Name (print) _____
Institution _____
Street _____
City/State/ZIP_____